Copyrighted & Trademarked Material

ISBN: 0692786767

TABLE OF CONTENTS

SECTION 4: "STOP THE PRESSES" .68

SECTION 5: FOLLOW-UP 94

FOREWORD

For over three decades, VentureCapital.org *(formerly known as the Wayne Brown Institute)* has helped train and assist individuals through the rigors of entrepreneurship to . . .

Start. Find Money. Change the World.

And we've been quite successful at our mission: graduates of our educational programs and pitch events have gone on to raise over $10 billion in funding — in spite of the fact that we're not based in Silicon Valley, New York City or any other financial center.

As the President and CEO of VentureCapital.org for 30-plus years, I have worked with thousands of very bright professionals — individuals often blessed with insights that have, in fact, led them to *Change the World*. Unfortunately, I have found that expertise in the nuances of software development, the intricacies of the human cell or the frontiers of engineering does not guarantee expertise in other areas, including the critical aspect of deciphering and translating the facets of groundbreaking innovations into plain English that can be understood (and appreciated) by all.

Which leads me to David Politis.

I've known/worked with David for over 27 years now. More importantly, I have seen firsthand his uncanny ability to grasp the nuances and implications of complicated concepts, products and services, while delivering *on point* Publicity messages and campaigns that help companies drive sales, recruit partners, attract investors, and boost the value of these enterprises. To be clear, his expertise is not limited to the realm of Publicity, but also includes all aspects of Public Relations, Investor Relations, Marketing, digital media and more.

But in the fields of Publicity, media relations and public relations — David stands above the rest. He is also an excellent coach, counselor and instructor, especially for those entrepreneurs who are new to the ins and outs of what it takes to generate ***Publicity Success***.

That is why I am honored to pen this Foreword for <u>66 RULES for Publicity Success</u>. From RULE #1 about *The Betty Factor* to RULE #66 about *Crisis Communication Plans*, this book is chock-full of specific details on the who, what, when, where, why and how of successful Publicity programs. Yet rather than approach this subject for PR or Marketing professionals, David has written <u>66 RULES for Publicity Success</u> for the inventors, entrepreneurs, creators and business owners of the world. In other words, this book is ideal for the vast majority of entrepreneurs we work with at VentureCapital.org on a daily basis — individuals who know exactly what they're doing when it comes to their area of expertise, but are typically at a loss when it comes to the world of Publicity.

So with my hearty recommendation, I invite you to use the RULES found within these pages as your guide to achieve ***Publicity Success***. They will help you understand and implement the Publicity actions required to boost the value of your firm as customers, partners, investors, employees and others act in ways that benefit you, your company and its owners.

Brad Bertoch
President & CEO
VentureCapital.org

ACKNOWLEDGEMENTS

Although I've often said I've got an idea for a book (or two) bouncing around in my head, the reality is that transforming such ideas into the written form has taken a LOT longer than I had ever anticipated.

But here it is, finally done, but not without help from many people.

First, I send out thanks to my favorite professors at Brigham Young University for helping me build a solid foundation in the overarching principles of Mass Communications, especially Ray Beckham, Ph.D. (my valued second PR Advisor) and Mark Stoddard (for revealing the mysteries of Direct Mail Writing), as well as Gaylen Jackson and Rulon Bradley, Ph.D.

Secondly, I express gratitude for all of my bosses, co-workers, and employees during my agency career, from Palo Alto to Seattle and from Salt Lake City to Draper, including colleagues and friends at Tycer-Fultz-Bellack, TFB/Davis, Dahlin Smith White, DSW Public Relations, Politis Communications, and SOAR Communications. I also express appreciation for the opportunity to transition into the corporate world as Chief Marketing Officer for ISYS Technologies, Xi3 Corporation and MULTIVOICE; what exciting, challenging and fulfilling times from late 2010 through early 2016!

Naturally, agency life is not complete without clients, and I have been blessed to work with many wonderful professionals during the past 30-*plus* years. Obviously there are too many to name individually within these pages. But of particular note, I extend special thanks to such individuals as Nathan Schulhof,

66 RULES for Publicity Success

Rich Linder, Hunter Jackson, Barb Patterson, Kenji Haroutunian, Jeff Oscodar, David Schulhof, Lance King, Brad Bertoch, Dan Young, Kathy Keenan, Dan Bellack, and Peter Horan, just to name a few.

Thanks too to the many friends and family members who provided great help in preparing 66 RULES for Publicity Success for publication, including editing and proofreading assistance, along with general feedback, from Jim Butler, T.C. Doyle, and Rob Vickery, among several others. I also extend a special shout-out to Shelby Winkel for copyediting this book. Bravo!

In addition, eternal thanks goes out to my wonderfully talented daughter, Alexi Politis, for her amazing work in the design and layout of this book. And of course, without the continued love and support of my fantastic wife, Allisha, I don't know that I would have ever finished 66 RULES for Publicity Success.

So . . . thank you, thank you, thank you. Now it's time to begin writing my next book.

PREFACE

In answer to questions from several friends about 66 RULES for Publicity Success, I offer the following answers:

This book is designed for entrepreneurs, inventors, business owners, scientists, creators and the like. These individuals, in their respective fields, are obviously very, very smart people. In fact, they are generally recognized as subject-matter experts, people who really know their stuff when it comes to electrical engineering, healthcare, Software-as-a-Service, physiology, telecommunications, auto repair and any other number of very technical fields.

Unfortunately, for many such very smart professionals, the basics of Marketing, let alone the specifics of Publicity and what it takes to produce ***Publicity Success***, remain a mystery to them. And that's not good.

It's not good because unless such brilliant individuals can understand and apply the various Publicity RULES found within these pages, they will find themselves, their creations and their companies severely hampered. Unfortunately, such hampering can prevent them and their inventions from achieving their full potential. {*And to be clear, from my perspective, a creation doesn't have to be a technology, per se, to be quite technical, such as a new way to prepare food or a new type of retailing.*}

Nevertheless, during my career, I have seen countless C-Level technologists, scientists, inventors and more transform their businesses because they leveraged Publicity RULES to their advantage. As a result, they drove new action with customers, partners, investors, employees, Journalists and influencers, which, in the end, helped increase the value of their companies, products, services and inventions.

In other words, <u>66 RULES for Publicity Success</u> helps readers learn how to

Drive Action & Boost Value.

That's the simple explanation. The details? They're inside these pages.

Hopefully, by the time you're done reading this book you will agree.

Dave Politis

= =

DEFINITIONS

Publicity *(pub-LISS-i-tee)*:

1. *The act of gaining or attracting extensive mention in the news media or by word of mouth or other means of communication* (Dictionary.com)

2. *The notice or attention given to someone or something by the media* (OxfordDictionaries.com)

3. *An act or device designed to attract public interest; specifically — information with news value issued as a means of gaining public attention or support* (Merriam-Webster Dictionary)

4. *Gaining public visibility or awareness for a product, service, company or person via the media* (Wikipedia)

Publicity — *The David Politis definition:*

The act or process of generating positive media coverage (aka, stories, reviews, mentions, etc.) about you, your invention, creation, product, service, cause, client and/or company/organization through any media outlet, e.g.,

- *Traditional Media (aka, print or broadcast),*
- *New Media (aka, online/digital/Website/Blogs),*
- *Social Media (platforms and services), and*
- *Customer/Partner Media (Websites, Blogs, Social Media, etc.), as well as*
- *Media Outlets that you Own, Control and/or Use,*

with the overarching goal of moving individuals and organizations to positive action that increases your value or the value of your company/organization and/or products/services.

66 RULES for Publicity Success

Publicity Success — *The David Politis definition:*

Although the end goals/objectives of Publicity Campaigns are unique to each organization/individual that undertakes such programs, successful Publicity campaigns should assist in the process of driving positive action for said organization/individual, with these positive actions being driven, in part, by positive media coverage. Such actions can range from Social Media "Likes" to testing new products/services or from signing petitions to buying stock in a company.

In turn, these actions concurrently boost the value of said organizations/individuals, either incrementally or dramatically. Hence,

$$\textit{Positive Media Coverage} \Rightarrow \textit{Positive Action} \Rightarrow$$
$$\textit{Increased Valuation} = \textit{Publicity Success}$$

Publicity 1.0 — *The David Politis definition:*

Targeted efforts to generate media coverage with traditional media outlets, either print- or broadcast-based (e.g., radio — including terrestrial and satellite; or television — cable, satellite and/or through-the-air). Since the mid-1990s, such efforts included story placement on the Websites of these traditional media outlets.

Publicity 2.0 — *The David Politis definition:*

Expands upon the focus noted in **Publicity 1.0** *to include targeted efforts to generate media coverage in online-only media properties, organizations that began to appear in the mid- to late-1990s, such as* CNET, MarketWatch, *and* TheStreet.com *(to name a few). Such Websites were and are invariably* **owned** *by the media outlets themselves or by a publishing company versus properties built upon platforms* **leased** *or* **rented** *by said media outlets or publishing companies, including Blogs or Social Media accounts.*

Publicity 3.0 — *The David Politis definition:*

> *Expands upon the focus noted in **Publicity 1.0** and **2.0** to include targeted efforts to generate media coverage in online-only media properties based on platforms the organizations <u>do not own</u> but rather **lease** or **rent**, including Social Media accounts ranging from* YouTube *channels to* Snapchat *accounts and from* Facebook *Pages to* LinkedIn *Profiles.*

> ***Publicity 3.0** also includes efforts to target media coverage by self-appointed Citizen-Journalists.*

> *Additionally, **Publicity 3.0** recognizes the fact that the evolving technological landscape has made it possible for any organization of any size (even those with limited resources), to become its own publishing company. As a result, organizations are now able to directly communicate with targeted audience members, bypassing traditional and non-traditional media outlets and publishing companies and do so via media properties that they own (e.g., Websites, podcasts, webcasts, etc.) or those that they **lease/rent**, including accounts with* Instagram, Snapchat, Pinterest *and others.*

= =

PROLOGUE

The Intern and the Tinkerer

"I may not be in Kansas, but it sure seems like it," Jerome thought as he remembered Dorothy's line from The Wizard of Oz. *He felt so far from his freshman dorm at the University of Miami, half a country away and four-plus years ago.*

It wasn't his fault he'd been assigned Ethanol as one of his beats, but interns didn't get to be choosy. At least that's what his one professor had told 'em over and over again. "You take what you're given, and then you do the best you can," she'd said.

Still, he wasn't surprised at the look on his editor's face when he pitched him his story idea, something about an alternate energy source from cow manure, a short item he'd dug up in the story archives from 20-plus years ago. No wonder his editor was skeptical.

But here he was at the T-intersection, blacktop stretching off into the distance behind his 12-year-old, mostly black Civic. Off to his right, the asphalt rolled out toward the horizon before it dipped behind a small rise a half mile down the road. And there through the bug-splattered windshield was the unpaved dirt road before him, just as the very pregnant clerk had said back at the weather-beaten country store.

A few minutes later he had a half-full Orange Fanta bottle in his hand as he sat on the passenger seat of a Razer side-by-side next to the silvery haired Mrs. Tompson. With beige dust kicking up in the air as they rounded a corner, the glint of the sun surprised him as it reflected off the low-lying shop roof. "Robert's in there," she shouted over the revving engine while pointing to the sliding barn door. As they slowed to a stop, the arthritic head of the Golden Retriever tilted slightly upward at their arrival, but the dog didn't move to get up, content to simply lie there in the shadows.

Then he was there, ambling toward them through the doorway in his grime-and oil-splattered lite-gray coveralls, a Denver Broncos ballcap protecting his head and clear safety glasses dangling around his neck.

"Hi, Mama," he said as he neared the Razer, the arch in his eyebrows asking the question his words did not.

"Robert, this is Jerome. He's from the paper. Says he's interested in your box. You know, the one we use with the cows?"

The old man's head turned ever so slightly as he looked disbelievingly at Jerome. "What had it been, 20 years?" the inventor wondered, thinking back to that day eons ago when he had first started up that contraption and two hours later diesel fuel had trickled out of the spigot. "Was it possible someone finally believed him?"

"Sir, I heard you built something, something that might be worth taking a look at. Do you mind telling me about it?"

Jerome extended his hand as he stepped off the four-wheeler, a hopeful look on his face. Robert glanced down briefly, then back up at the expectant face before him and smiled as he embraced Jerome's hand in his.

"Sure thing, kid. What'd you say your name was?"

"Jerome."

"Well come around back, Jerome. I'm not sure if it's worth the trip all the way out here or not, but I'll show you what I've done."

The two of them began down the dry dirt path away from the shop as Mrs. Tompson restarted the Razer.

"And where'd you say you're from?" Robert asked, his cracked work boots creating mini dust clouds as they walked.

2

"The paper, the one in Dubuque."

"Uhh, okay. Here it is."

Robert spread his arms wide in front of them, palms upward, as if he were a symphony conductor ready to begin a command performance. There stood a pickup-sized metal box with a 2x2-foot opening in the middle of the side they were facing, while on the path-side a one-inch spigot extruded a foot away from the contraption.

"I left Miami for this?" Jerome wondered. "Wow."

= =

INTRODUCTION

When you first explain to them that you have started on your entrepreneurial journey, friends, loved ones, professors, wizened sages, investors, and even strangers will each dip into their communal bag of clichéd sayings to try and encourage you. When they do, chances are they will say something like this:

If you build a better mousetrap, the world will beat a path to your door.
Anonymous

Clearly, they mean well. Unfortunately, *Anonymous* was wrong. And that's a problem, a really big problem. It's also why I decided to write this book.

Since finishing my Mass Communications studies at Brigham Young University over 30 years ago, I have worked with thousands of very, very bright people, each of whom had invented (or was a member of the team that invented — or created) — the next big thing. In some regard, each new invention was the equivalent of the *better mousetrap* for that respective industry.

These inventions typically fell into markets ranging from electronics to software and from recreation to transportation, while their inventors/creators ranged from people holding Ph.D. and MD degrees to a few who had barely graduated from high school. In each instance, however, they were clearly *Subject-Matter Experts*. And often, that was their biggest problem: their subject-matter expertise.

4

Case in point, why is it that your primary care physician will use the phrase *deep contusion* to describe what's wrong with your kid instead of saying your child has a deep bruise? Sticking with medical terminology for a moment, you might also have an MD tell you that your mother suffered a *myocardial infarction* instead of just saying that she had a heart attack.

Why is that? And is this just a problem with the medical field? {*The answer to the second question is "No," but more about the answers to both questions in a bit.*}

What I've come to understand and appreciate is that the more technical the field, the greater the likelihood that that particular industry will have its own lingua franca, its own terminology for providing verbal- and written-shorthand that is used by the practitioners within their field. And when one industry professional is speaking with another, such terms and acronyms serve as a crucial form of shorthand, enabling a lot of information to be communicated very quickly.

Unfortunately, the use of such industry-specific terminology also increases the chances that these practitioners will use the same words and phrases with everyone and not just with their industry colleagues, such as conversations among doctors, nurses, radiologists and others in healthcare. I suspect that in most cases this is because they forget that not everyone speaks the same language as they do; conversely, it may just be because they assume that we understand their acronym-driven, highfalutin' language.

Unfortunately, we don't.

Additionally, when these really smart people envision something that has never been imagined or done before, they often have an amazing clarity about their new thing, their invention. And with that vision in mind they set to work to create or build what they have already seen in their mind's eye.

Regrettably, most of them have a really difficult time translating into plain English what they have envisioned or they are challenged to do so in such a way that allows others to begin to grasp their world-changing creation. Even more paradoxically, most inventors falsely believe that their invention/creation is, in fact, a *better mousetrap*, and because he/she has invented a *better mousetrap*, surely the world will beat a pathway to their door, right?

That's the conundrum that my fictional Robert faced in the story excerpt at the beginning of this book. He had invented a single-farm system for converting cow manure into diesel fuel, a system that produced more energy than required to run it. And the system did work, up to a point, which was why there had been a story published about Robert. But the energy conversion ratio at the time had been modest, and interest in his invention, such as it was, evaporated overnight.

So . . . even though Robert had continued to work on and perfect his invention (and no doubt, it had gotten better), the world had not *beaten a path to his door*. In fact, the world had forgotten about Robert and his invention, and it most certainly did not even remember where his door was anymore. Until Jerome came around.

The purpose of <u>66 RULES for Publicity Success</u> is to help ensure that you never end up like Robert. In fact, this book is designed to help you identify and attract the attention of the Jeromes and Jessies of the world — Journalists looking for the next breaking story, perhaps even that story that will win them the Pulitzer Prize.

As a business owner, inventor, entrepreneur and/or creator reading this book, you have built (or are building) something special. Will it transform the entire world? Perhaps. Or perhaps just a small piece of the planet.

Unfortunately, if you expect the world to *beat a pathway to your door* simply because you have imagined something wonderful, the reality is that you will likely wait a very, very long time. Thankfully, there are things that you can do and steps that you can take to ensure that you

- Get the credit you deserve (both within your industry and from the world at large),
- Attract the right customers, partners, employees and/or investors,
- Drive sales, and
- Boost the value of your creation/invention.

The easiest and least expensive way to accomplish your goals and objectives for your business/invention is though Publicity, which in reality is a subset of "Media Relations," which in turn is part of the practice of "Public Relations."

66 RULES for Publicity Success takes everything I have learned in my 30-plus-year career and boils it down into a simple-to-follow set of RULES that anyone can understand and adapt to their unique circumstances and creation.

In **SECTION 1** of this book you will come to understand the biggest mistake nearly every inventor makes and learn how to overcome it. You'll then learn how to translate your big idea into a simple, encapsulated image or statement that can be used with anyone, without minimizing the *better mousetrap* you have created.

In **SECTION 2** of this book I focus on the various publics (or target audiences) you will try to reach, with a special emphasis on Journalists — the key professionals that will help you garner the ***Publicity Success*** you crave and need.

Next, in **SECTION 3** of 66 RULES for Publicity Success you will find detailed descriptions of six key types of documents and files you will need on your journey — materials Journalists find absolutely critical in performing their jobs. In addition, I outline a key yet simple mistake many organizations make in their Media Relations programs, a mistake you will be able to avoid.

SECTION 4 takes us to the heart of any Publicity campaign, the place where the "rubber meets the road." In this section, I provide an overview of what I see as the *Journalist Mindset*, a perspective I believe is critical to achieving ***Publicity Success***. In addition, I walk you through important aspects of why and how you should package-up news, information and data about your invention, creation, business, etc. into the proper formats for working with Journalists of all types, from Reporters to Editors and from Bloggers to Producers. This Section also takes on the sometime scary proposition of "pitching" a story idea to a media outlet and provides you with specific RULES to use when you're ready to begin sharing your story with Journalists.

SECTION 5 of 66 RULES for Publicity Success continues the process started in Section 4 by examining ways to overcome rejection {*because it will happen*}, as well as steps to take to improve your likelihood of generating the Publicity results you hope to achieve. You'll also find a handful of recommendations in this section about how to leverage your ***Publicity Success***.

SECTION 6 is my effort to make sense of **Publicity 3.0** — that world where any individual/organization can be (and is) his, her or its own media company, all courtesy of the World Wide Web and the explosion of Social Media services and platforms. This tectonic shift in the media world has broad-ranging implications for everyone, but especially for those interested in achieving ***Publicity Success***.

The role of advanced planning and the setting of Publicity ground RULES is the focus of **SECTION 7**, something I've named "**Think Before You . . .**", while **SECTION 8** is centered on other tools and platforms you should deploy in your various Publicity campaigns, including Commercial Wire Services, Media Alerts, Press Tours and more. Conversely, **SECTION 9** contains a series of Miscellaneous RULES that don't fit neatly into any other area of the book, so I grouped them together into their own separate section.

"From Pennies to Millions" is a Case Study I use to provide a concrete example of how the right Publicity campaign can transform a business, followed by concluding thoughts on how the RULES and ideas found in this book can help you achieve the goals and objectives ***you have set*** for your business, invention and/or creation — whatever those goals and objectives may be.

So . . . welcome to 66 RULES for Publicity Success; I hope you like it. More importantly, I hope you find it helpful, if not transformational.

And please let me know what you think about this book and its RULES. I've set up a special email account for that very purpose: 66RULESfor.PublicitySuccess@gmail.com. {*Apologies in advance that the address is so long.*} But seriously, feel free to write. But for now, on to the rest of the book.

= =

SECTION 1: POSITIONING & MESSAGING

In his bestselling-book <u>The Seven Habits of Highly Effective People</u> Stephen R. Covey uses Habit #2 to teach how critical it is for individuals to "Begin with the End in Mind." In this Habit, Covey explains the invaluable importance of something I call "Creation Squared" — the concept that success typically comes from creating something in your mind first and then creating that same thing again in the physical world.

I believe this same concept is an intrinsic cog in the process of achieving success in any business — the need to "Begin with the End in Mind."

And so it is for you.

What is it that you hope to achieve by reading this book? Do you fully understand the purpose of your business? And the purposes served (or delivered) by your products/services?

Similarly, who are the various publics that you serve? And why? And what is it about your products (and/or services) that make them unique enough (or valuable enough) to certain individuals that they will buy <u>stuff</u> from your enterprise?

Better yet, can you answer the preceding questions in such a way that a perspective customer or investor **_not_** from your industry will understand your answers so clearly, so compellingly, that he or she would want to buy from you? Or invest in your company?

66 RULES for Publicity Success

The RULES within this section are each designed to provide foundational concepts to help you achieve ***Publicity Success***, which (in turn) will help you achieve greater results with your business. In fact, without understanding and then applying these RULES properly, I believe that you will dramatically hamper your ability to drive action and increase the value of your enterprise.

Conversely, as you grasp the underlying purposes and principles of the RULES within this section, I believe you will find it relatively easy to adapt the concepts these RULES contain to allow you to successfully address your specific situation, challenges and opportunities.

= = = = = = = = = = = = = = = = = = = =

RULE #1: Utilize *The Betty Factor*

I first met Betty Benton Mann in the summer of 1981, a few months before she became my mother-in-law.

A former dental technician and the mother of five kids, Betty was like most women of the Great Depression:

- She took care of things around the home,
- Did the shopping, cleaning and cooking,
- Was involved in church activities, and
- Did her best to keep the home fires burning while her husband, Ray, was away on business.

In other words, Betty was primarily a stay-at-home mom.

What she was not, however, was a technologist. Not by a long shot.

One summer in the mid-1990s, Betty and Ray got their first home computer. The occasion? Betty had been asked by her local church leaders to perform some volunteer genealogical work, work that required having a computer.

Although the IBM personal computer had been introduced more than a dozen years earlier, Betty had never worked with a PC before. So she had questions — lots of 'em.

One evening my wife, Allisha, related to me an experience that she had had earlier in the day with her mom.

Betty had called all upset, virtually on the edge of tears. Apparently she had been working on her computer on some big project when a neighbor stopped by for a short visit.

When Betty returned to her home office some 20 minutes later, her long hard work had disappeared.

"It's gone," she sobbed into the phone. "It's all gone."

Trying to ascertain the situation across town, Allisha started with the basics of computer support. "Tell me what you see on the screen, Mom."

"Nothing," she stated dejectedly. "It's black. Just black."

I smiled knowingly as Allisha related her tale.

"Really?" I asked Allisha.

"Yeah, really."

Allisha then explained what happened next.

"Mom," she asked, "do you see your computer mouse sitting next to your computer? Just slide it around on the top of your desk."

Moments later, an excited squeal was heard through the phone line. "What happened? What did you do?"

Allisha then patiently explained the concept of screensavers to her mom and how automatically darkening a computer monitor helped prevent burning out pixels on the monitor.

Later that evening as I contemplated Betty's *aha moment*, I realized that the fact that she didn't know about this hidden software feature or how it worked didn't mean that Betty was stupid. It simply meant that she didn't know.

This idea made me ponder about all of the new gadgets, gizmos, products and services I had helped promote and market over the years. Some of these had been targeted at savvy technologists, others at consumers.

In each instance, however, the new *thing* had delivered new capabilities previously unavailable, and in some instances, previously unimaginable.

For example, the Rubicon Filter from Rubicon Medical allowed specialized heart surgeons to capture dangerous flecks of sludge inside blood vessels after a stenting procedure to open clogged arteries. This was an entirely innovative approach to removing such embolic material and preventing dangerous medical events like kidney failure or stroke.

On the other end of the spectrum, audiohighway's Listen Up Player was the first patent-pending handheld device that allowed people to play back songs and audio recordings that had been purchased and downloaded from the Internet — a forerunner to today's ubiquitous MP3 players and smartphones. In fact, by the time its assets were purchased by Sony out of bankruptcy proceedings, audiohighway and its founder, Nathan Schulhof, had been issued four U.S. patents, each surrounding and protecting the systems and methodologies for digitally acquiring, cataloging, selling and delivering audio content to consumers' handheld devices via the Internet.

As I considered the features and benefits of these and countless other products I had helped launch and/or promote and the fact that they had often delivered new (and in some instances never previously contemplated) features and benefits, I realized that my professional challenge had always been formulating new ways for explaining new things.

In fact, I came to realize that <u>my greatest successes during my career had always come when I had simplified our Messaging</u> to the point that anyone could understand the benefits and features of a new thing. This was especially true for those creations that were especially *geeky* or technical.

And that was the key.

I merely had to simplify the message so that anyone, regardless of their technical background, training or profession could understand the capabilities and results of any new thing. Then if the message recipient had a more technical background, I found we could always take a more technical approach, so that wasn't a problem either.

In fact, my personal breakthrough was understanding that if I always approached Messaging with my mother-in-law in mind, I would never have a problem in communicating the benefits and features of new products, services or companies. And at the end of the day that meant more money for my clients and for me, as well as greater benefits for end-users as they adopted these new products and/or services.

Simply put, **if Betty** *"got it,"* **so would everyone else**. And if Betty did not understand, then I needed to go back to the drawing board until I came up with a better explanation, definition and/or message. And if that required getting more technical in my Messaging, I knew I could do that too.

Some people might suggest that this concept was already embodied in the acronym K-I-S-S: *Keep It Simple, Stupid.* And they might be right.

But as someone who works with technical people, products, services and companies every day, this epiphany was critical and has shaped my PR and Marketing philosophies ever since. That's why I call it *The Betty Factor.*

For the record, this RULE will be one of the longest of the RULES within this book. But in some ways that's because it is *THE foundational idea* behind each of the individual RULES described within <u>66 RULES for Publicity Success</u>.

Since that Betty-led epiphany roughly 20 years ago, I have discovered that virtually every profession requires a level of technical understanding to be truly successful, and I do mean virtually every profession, not just the obvious ones. This includes

- Window-washing, and
- Tailoring, and
- Landscaping, and
- Tutoring, and
- Auto Repair, and
- Retailing, and
- Transportation, and
- Banking, and
- Interior Design, and
- Cattle Ranchers, and
- Healthcare, and
- On and on and on and on.

According to the 2010 U.S. Census, there are more than 27 million small businesses within the United States, and this book is written for each and every one of those businesses and their owners. Here's why:

The more technical or complex the products and/or services provided by a company, the more critical it becomes to be able to communicate clearly and succinctly the benefits and features of those products/services to prospective customers, partners, employees, investors and more. And for you (the business owner, entrepreneur, inventor, general manager and/or creator), this is especially true if others do not have the same technical know-how or expertise as you do.

In other words, you have to be able to explain the benefits and features of your products, services, inventions, creations and/or business to Betty, or

- To your Uncle George, or
- To your neighbor Shawna, or
- To your friend Tom,
- Etc.

And until you can do this — *take a complex subject and boil it down to its most salient and compelling facts so that someone outside your industry will understand at least the basics* — you will fail in your efforts to achieve ***Publicity Success***.

This is the overarching concept behind *The Betty Factor*. Understanding this idea and being able to apply *The Betty Factor* to your business, your products and/or your services is absolutely crucial.

Learn to do this and you will be well on your way to ***Publicity Success***. Fail to do this and you will struggle.

= =

RULE #2: It's ALL about Positioning & Messaging

Does the short list below bring back any memories for you?

- A
- B
- C
- A + B
- B + C
- A + C
- All of the above
- None of the above

Yup, it's a set of possible answers to a question from a multiple choice test.

For me, multiple choice questions were sometimes the hardest ones to answer during a test. Why? That's easy: Because they required a comprehensive understanding of the subject.

The same is also true when it comes to Positioning and Messaging. Even if you've sussed-out a topic to the point so you can . . .

> *boil it down to its most salient and compelling facts so that a person outside your industry will understand at least the basics . . .*

that does NOT mean you have accomplished the task of properly crafting the Positioning and Messaging for that complex subject. {*Although, to be frank, if you can explain a technical something so your Grandpa Bob can understand it, chances are you are well on your way to* Betty Factor *success as well.*}

Unfortunately, just because YOU can explain a technical something so that others will understand its "basics" does not mean that anyone else in your organization can do the same thing. And that's the difference.

Specifically, in order for *The Betty Factor* to truly work, you should be able to get others to take what you have learned and share it with other people, whether they are company insiders or complete strangers. That's where Positioning and Messaging come into play.

And although both are typically joined-at-the-hip, let's consider both exercises separately at first.

POSITIONING

As of this writing, *Dictionary.com*'s first definition for the word Position (as a noun) is as follows:

> *Condition with reference to place; location; situation.*

And as a verb, *Dictionary.com* further defines Position as

> *To put in a particular or appropriate position; place.*

Taken together, I believe a more comprehensive meaning of Positioning is being able to define and/or describe where something or someone **_IS_** relative to other similar or competing things or people.

For example, if I showed you a written list of the Top 10 Automobile Brands registered in New York City by women, could you position each brand relative to the others on that list? If so, chances are you might create something like the Chart on the following page.

19

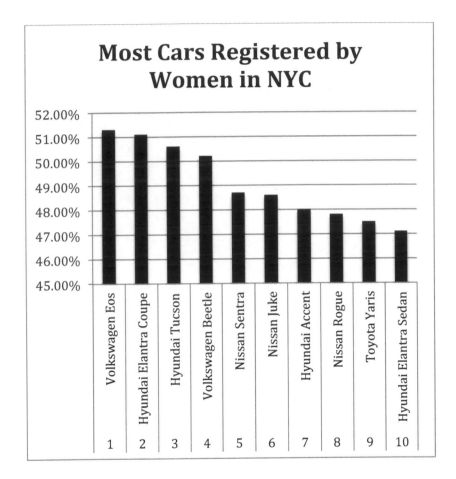

Conversely, that same data outlined into a written ranking could look like this:

	Ranking of the Most Cars Registered by Women in New York City	
1	Volkswagen Eos	51.30%
2	Hyundai Elantra Coupe	51.10%
3	Hyundai Tucson	50.60%
4	Volkswagen Beetle	50.20%
5	Nissan Sentra	48.70%
6	Nissan Juke	48.60%
7	Hyundai Accent	48.00%
8	Nissan Rogue	47.80%
9	Toyota Yaris	47.50%
10	Hyundai Elantra Sedan	47.10%

Both examples — the Chart on the previous page and the list above — are each examples of Positioning. How? Because both explain, describe or show automobile ownership percentages of women in New York City.

Clearly there are other methods that can be used when it comes to Positioning. However, I believe the primary purpose of Positioning is to

*define and/or describe where something or someone **IS** relative to other similar or competing things or people.*

Which leads us to the role of Messaging.

MESSAGING

Just because you can "define and/or describe where something or someone IS relative to other similar or competing things or people" does not mean that other people can do the same thing. That's why you need Messaging.

I believe that the best Marketing definition of Messaging is:

> *The act of capturing the audible, visual or written definition and/or description of something (or someone) relative to other similar or competing things or people.*

In other words, your Messaging is **_NOT_** done until it is

- Written down,
- Created visually, and/or
- Captured as an audible recording.

Why? Because Messaging is meant to be shared with (and ideally BY) other people. This includes

- Employees,
- Investors,
- Customers,
- Partners,
- Politicians,
- Retailers, and
- Others.

In other words, Messaging that is done well allows you to leverage what you have sussed-out through your *Betty Factor* and Positioning exercises about your product, service, company, invention or "what have you" so that you can accomplish two things:

22

1. Be able to communicate the exact same messages again and again to other people (or organizations),
2. So you can get ___THEM___ to share the same, exact messages again and again to other people (or organizations).

And that leads us to the intersecting beauty of *The Betty Factor*, Positioning and Messaging:

Leveraged Replication.

In other words, with Leveraged Replication you can take what you have created with your Messaging, Positioning and *Betty Factor* endeavors and transfer your creations to other people, simply and easily. As a result, you can make sure of two things:

1. That you communicate the exact same message(s) again and again. You can also be assured that
2. Other people and organizations will also precisely and accurately communicate the same exact message(s) again and again.

To be clear, chances are your initial efforts at *"Betty-fying"* your product, service, company, invention, etc. through this process will likely result in Positioning and Messaging platforms and statements that are too long, too big and/or too broad. That's okay. Almost everyone has a similar struggle of producing too much to begin with.

It is, however, the process of re-examining, refining and editing your initial efforts at Messaging and Positioning that excellence can be found — which leads us to the next several RULES.

= =

BONUS RULE: *Plan, Plan, Plan*

{**NOTE**: In addition to the formal 66 RULES found within this book, I have added in a handful of BONUS RULES — *like this one* —that I felt added incremental value and were too important to keep out of these pages. I hope you agree.}

= = = = = = = = = = = = = = = =

There's a fairly famous cliché that reads:

If you fail to plan, you plan to fail.

And why is this statement a cliché? Because it's true.

As much as it might be nice to believe that planning alone will remove all mistakes and lead to a happy La-La Land of Publicity Nirvana, the reality is that planning alone will NOT do that. But it will definitely help.

It's likely you already have an overall Business Plan in place for your company, as well as a Marketing/Sales Plan. If not, then I'd recommend you set this book aside until you've got both in place, at least in outline form.

However, even if you have previously prepped a Business Plan and a Marketing/Sales Plan, chances are you've not prepared a separate Publicity Plan. But that's okay, because it's a fairly straightforward process to create one — at least it will be as you go through this book.

And now that we've examined the importance of The Betty Factor, *the critical nature of both Positioning and Messaging, as*

24

well as many of the foundational tools for Publicity campaigns, it's time to get started.

Clearly, since you've just begun reading <u>66 RULES for Publicity Success</u>, *I don't expect you'll know all the ins and outs necessary to craft a Publicity or Media Relations Plan. But . . . you can begin the process.*

Besides, IF you will take the time in advance to create a Publicity Plan (or Media Relations Plan), chances are <u>greatly increased</u> *that*

A.   ***You will be successful***, *and*
B.   ***You will NOT screw-up***, *whether in ways large or small.*

This means you will generate the **Publicity Success** *you really want and need. And that sounds like a very worthwhile outcome to me. In other words:*

Plan, Plan, Plan.

   = = = = = = = = = = = = = = = = = = =

RULE #3: Create a Verbal Elevator Pitch *(30 Seconds or Less)*

Venture capitalists call it the **"Elevator Pitch."**

Simply put, an **Elevator Pitch** means that you can explain what your company, product or service does — *and how it's better than competing offerings* — in 30 seconds or less. When you're done crafting your **Elevator Pitch**, everyone — *including your grandma* — should understand what the heck it is you're talking about.

If not, you should go back to the drawing board.

Simplify. Demystify. Then start over again, especially if you're trying to describe a technical product, service or process. {*And by technical, I'm not just referring to the latest software application or technology gizmo. Any job or field that requires special training or a college degree by definition means having at least some level of technical know-how, and if that's the case, chances are you need an* **Elevator Pitch**.}

Begin by trying to write a simple, easy-to-understand **Elevator Pitch** that can be spoken in <u>30 seconds or less</u>. Then share verbally what you've written with someone who is NOT in your industry. If that person understands it, great. If not, try again.

Remember . . . the goal here is to produce a short, to-the-point, easy-to-understand definition that can be spoken in less than 30 seconds.

Additionally, please resist the temptation to try and cram everything into this one **Elevator Pitch**, especially since you can always get more technical later.

= = = = = = = = = = = = = = = = = = = =

RULE #4: Produce a Written Elevator Pitch *(50 Words or Fewer)*

If you can pass the **Elevator Pitch** process {*that fun test thrown at entrepreneurs by venture capitalists*}, and you are able to tell someone about the unique benefits of your product or service in 30 seconds or less, surely you can highlight the essence of that same product or service in 50 words or less, right?

And when you're done and have got everything nailed just right, you shared it with your grandma, right? At least you shared it with someone outside your industry, correct?

If not, keep writing. And editing. At least until you have captured the beneficial essence of your product, service or process into 50 words or less. And then, once your written description can be easily understood by someone who is NOT an engineer or doctor or scientist (or appropriate industry-specific expert), then you're ready to move forward.

Precisely. Succinctly. Clearly.

In summary:

> *Being able to describe in writing given products,*
> *services, technologies, processes, sciences and the*
> *like is a key aspect of any successful Publicity program.*

In other words, this is the written version of an Elevator Pitch. And EVERY company needs one . . . whether it plans to raise money from investors or not.

= = = = = = = = = = = = = = = = = = = =

SECTION 2: IT'S ALL ABOUT THEM

> *A lot of times, people don't know what*
> *they want until you show it to them.*
> Steve Jobs

It's easy to agree that the mercurial co-founder of Apple was absolutely correct with his statement above. Then again, it would be absolutely incorrect to suggest that Steve Jobs was the sole arbiter of good and bad or right and wrong.

I believe that every business owner interested in gaining market share is always concerned about the tastes and interests of his/her customers and other target audiences. Such is the case in pursuing ***Publicity Success***.

If you believe as I do that succeeding in the world of media relations can help you achieve greater success in business, then it stands to reason that you must learn to understand and know your customers, including those customers known as Journalists. {***NOTE****: From my perspective, Journalists do qualify as prospective customers for your company, even if they don't actually buy something from you with money. The difference is that Journalists typically use time and their expertise as their currency. Hence, for the purpose of this book, I consider Journalists as prospective or current customers.*}

That's why the RULES found within this section have been prepared specifically to help you identify and target the best Journalists for your Publicity campaigns.

= = = = = = = = = = = = = = = = = = = =

RULE #5: Know Your Customers

At its core, Public Relations involves identifying one or more targeted publics. Seems pretty obvious, right?

The same can also be said for Publicity and Media Relations programs.

BUT . . . if you have NOT identified (in advance) who you are targeting and why, you are destined to fail in your PR efforts.

For example, your campaign might be centered on reaching, educating and influencing

- graduating college seniors,
- single mothers,
- state legislators,
- retail investors,
- hourly employees, or
- 15- to 16-year-old girls living in Eugene, Oregon who do **not** watch the reality TV show *So You Think You Can Dance.*

Regardless, BEFORE you start any PR effort, you must know as much as possible about your targeted publics.

> *{NOTE: If it makes it more palatable to use the term "audiences" instead of "publics," please feel free to do so.}*

= = = = = = = = = = = = = = = = = = = =

RULE #6: Know the Media Your Customers "Consume"

Nearly everyone in the Public Relations/Marketing Communications industries understands that the publishing capabilities afforded by the Internet/Web have created tremendous pressure on traditional, mainstream media outlets, as shown by the ongoing headcount reductions in the media world.

Notwithstanding such pressure, there are still a ton of media outlets around the world, with new ones being born every day, especially if one includes Blogs within the definition of "media outlets."

This being the case, PR professionals know that their best media relations results are often garnered if they match story ideas to the right media outlet. And for you and your company, that means you need to know the various media outlets your customers "consume" (or use).

This holds true for

- Local media outlets (television, radio, newspapers, magazines and Blogs) — examples include *KGO-TV, WCBS-AM*, the *Miami Herald* and *UtahPolicy.com*;
- Business media outlets (local, national, specialty focused and Blogs) — examples include *St. Louis Business Journal, Forbes, Bicycle Retailer & Industry News* and *BeehiveStartups.com*;
- Trade media outlets (local, national and Blogs) — examples in the Marketing industry include *Adnews, Advertising Age* and *SearchEngineLand.com*;

- Consumer media outlets (local, national and Blogs) — examples include *D Magazine*, *O — The Oprah Magazine* and *TMZ*; and
- Special interest media outlets (local, national and Blogs) — examples include *Columns Magazine*, *Field & Stream* and *Engadget*.

Additionally, when it comes time to pitch a story idea, make sure you first consider what media outlets will best fit your story idea before moving forward.

= =

RULE #7: Know the Ideal <u>Type</u> of Journalist for You and Your Company *(Reporter, Feature Writer, Editor, Anchor, Columnist, Reviewer, Blogger, Podcaster, Etc.)*

For the record, it's NOT enough to identify the best media outlet for a story idea. You also have to identify the right Journalist.

That individual might be a

- Reporter,
- Editor,
- Producer,
- Anchor,
- Blogger, or
- Something else.

That Journalist might even have the title of Editorial Assistant. *{And yes, I am absolutely serious about this last suggestion.}*

How will you know?

- Check out the masthead (if one exists) and examine titles.
- Examine beats.
- Use a service like Cision, Agility, SourceBottle, Meltwater or others.
- Ask.

However, when it comes to targeting the most perfect Journalist to pitch, that involves hands-on research.

Primarily this means reading, watching and/or listening to past stories written or produced by the Journalist in question. Such efforts will not only show you the type of stories this professional writes/produces, but will also tell you if they tend to be

- Skeptical (in tone),
- Bring in outside sources (to lend an impartial slant to stories),
- Mention other companies in stories,
- Etc.

Taking the time to actually find and review such stories will help you absolutely, positively find the best Journalist for your story pitch.

Regardless, the better you target your pitch to the right Journalist, the better chance you will have for ***Publicity Success***.

= = = = = = = = = = = = = = = = = = = =

RULE #8: Conduct Keyword Searches to Identify Journalists You Can Target

Even if you use Agility, Cision or another online service to help you find and identify the best Journalist for a particular story pitch, you can speed up the process by using keyword searches.

Here's how to make this work for you:

- Presuming you have identified the "best" media outlet for your story idea, use the search feature on the outlet's home page and enter in the words or terms best aligned with your pitch.
- For example, if you work for (or represent) a company that's launching a new Web-based personal finance application, you could search for the terms "Web-based," "software" and/or "personal finance" on the media outlet's Website.
- The most recently published stories should then be reviewed to see which ones, if any, were actually produced by Journalists on staff and not by a Wire Service.
- If you find that several stories on the same subject(s) were written by the same reporter, chances are you've found the best Journalist for your story.

    {*NOTE: If there is no search function on a specific media outlet's Website, you can also generate useful results by entering the same words/terms (along with the name of the media outlet) in a* Google *search. For instance, using the example above, your search string for a Journalist working at* Fortune *might look like this:* Fortune.com *Web-based software "personal finance."*

In this example, I wanted to look for the actual phrase "personal finance" so I included it within quote marks. Doing so means a search engine will recognize it as a specific phrase.

Clearly, this approach is a bit more cumbersome, but it should work well enough, especially if a Website doesn't have a search function. }

= = = = = = = = = = = = = = = = = = = =

RULE #9: Leverage Social Media *(especially LinkedIn)* for Your Journalist Research

If (in your efforts to identify the perfect Journalist), you do NOT utilize Social Media, you are making a big mistake.

The majority of full-time Journalists and freelance writers have at least one public profile published somewhere within the bazillions of Social Media platforms used around the world. As part of your pre-pitch research, I strongly recommend utilizing these Social Media services.

For example, both Ed Baig (of *USA Today*) and Tom Harvey (of the *Salt Lake Tribune*) have public profiles on *LinkedIn.com*.

And although such public profiles are sometimes a bit Spartan, they can often provide valuable information — info that can lead to insights about how best to package-up a story idea prior to a formal pitch.

Another way to use Social Media when conducting media relations research is to determine topics Journalists are interested in or what their particular plans may be.

Case in point, while preparing to launch a new electric bicycle several years ago at the International CES trade show, my agency used *Twitter* to find and identify Journalists at a number of media outlets who

- Planned to attend CES, and
- Were looking for new green tech story ideas.

This effort alone landed us stories with *CNET*, *MSN* and *DVICE.com*, just to name a few.

In other words, *Twitter* and other Social Media platforms can also be used to locate Journalists who might be interested in your company, products and/or services.

> *{NOTE: Twitter has its own internal search capability. Simply go to https://search.twitter.com and then enter in the word or phrase you're looking for. Good luck.}*

= = = = = = = = = = = = = = = = = = =

BONUS RULE: Research Twitter Lists

> *A sometime overlooked tool for identifying targeted Journalists are* Twitter *Lists.*
>
> *Specifically, go to a Search Engine type in the following search words:*

- ### "twitter *lists*" *computer journalists*

> *When I did this moments ago, I got back more than 65,000 results. Click on virtually any of the resulting links and you'll be on your way to finding computer Journalists on Twitter, as well as Twitter Lists focused on other types of Journalists.*
>
> *Naturally, you can search for virtually any other category of Journalists via a Twitter Lists search.*

= = = = = = = = = = = = = = = = = = =

RULE #10: As a Last Resort, Ask for Help

If you're still having difficulty identifying the best Journalist for a particular story pitch, try contacting the **Editorial Assistant.**

This is a position you can often find on magazine staffs, but occasionally other media outlets also use Editorial Assistants as well.

Yes, this person will likely be one of the most junior people on the editorial staff. That's okay. Chances are they'll know who the best person is to contact with your story idea.

If, however, you're still at a loss at whom to pitch to at a given media outlet, and there is no Editorial Assistant on staff, try contacting the **Managing Editor**.

Most media outlets have at least one M.E. on their teams, even broadcast outlets.

Just recognize that Managing Editors tend to be very busy senior Journalists, so be brief and to the point when contacting an M.E., even if it's via an email.

= = = = = = = = = = – – – – – – – – – = = =

RULE #11: Smaller Journalist Databases are Better

One key trick to being successful at media relations is to make sure you <u>divide editorial contact databases into smaller segments.</u> Such segments can/should be based upon

- Beats covered (new products, sports, health, etc.),
- Title (reporter, reviewer, feature writer, etc.),
- Geography (city, state, region, country),
- Industry focus (personal computers, legal, athletics, women's issues, etc.),
- Media type (newspaper, online only, television, radio, etc.) or
- Another focus altogether.

Such segmentation will improve your chances for ***Publicity Success*** when pitching targeted story ideas, distributing News Releases, and crafting media relations strategies.

= = = = = = = = = = = = = = = = = = =

SECTION 3: BACKGROUND INFO AND TOOLS

After getting this far into <u>66 RULES of Publicity Success,</u> you've been encouraged to re-examine the Positioning and Messaging for your business and products/services from a new perspective — from the viewpoint of someone who is not a subject-matter expert in your field.

Perhaps that individual is your mother-in-law, as it was for me: Betty Mann. Or perhaps it's one of your neighbors.

But the overarching idea behind the first two sections of this book is to take the old saw to *"walk in someone else's shoes"* and apply it to your own Marketing and Publicity programs.

As you do this, clearly you need to understand your various *Publics:* this is the term public relations pros use to define "market segments" or "target audiences." Clearly this means your existing and prospective customers.

As a book focused on helping you to achieve ***Publicity Success***, obviously business owners need to focus much of their efforts on Journalists, especially on learning how to define, understand and target them.

So with RULES surrounding Messaging/Positioning and Publics behind us, it's now time to look at some of the top Tools you'll need for your Publicity campaigns. These Tools will help you provide the background information every Journalist craves, and that's the purpose behind this section.

= =

RULE #12: <u>Facts Sheets</u> are *Must Haves*

Here's a rhetorical question for you:

> *The purpose of* 66 RULES *for Publicity Success is to help you figure out how to be successful at Publicity, right?*

Right.

In that case, you have to know about <u>Facts Sheets</u> and learn how to use them as a regular part of your Publicity efforts.

Whether you are connecting with a Journalist for the first time or the 100th time, she or he needs a quick way to get up-to-speed on you, your organization, people, products, services, etc. And the fastest way for this to happen is with <u>Facts Sheets</u>.

<u>Facts Sheets</u> are

> *One-page documents that provide an easy-to-understand overview of a company, product, service, invention or person.*

Using this definition, clearly a <u>Facts Sheet</u> written for a company will differ from a <u>Facts Sheet</u> created for a service. However, when I'm pulling together a <u>Facts Sheet</u> for the first time, I always make sure that I answer the six most critical questions every Journalist asks when researching or producing a story, namely

- Who,
- What,
- When,
- Where,
- Why, and
- How.

When completed, <u>Facts Sheets</u> must include the following five items:

1. **A Title, Headline and/or Logo** (to clarify who/what each <u>Facts Sheet</u> is about),
2. **Publication Date** (to notify the reader as to how current the information is in that particular <u>Facts Sheet</u>),
3. **Subheads** (to make it easier for a Journalist to scan for the information he/she is most interested in reading),
4. **24x7x365 Contact Info**, and
5. **Page Numbers** (yes, even if your <u>Facts Sheet</u> is only one side of a single sheet of paper).

And although this may seem obvious to you, a <u>Facts Sheet</u> must be limited to a single sheet of paper, otherwise it's no longer a "Sheet," right? However, printing on both sides of a single sheet of paper is acceptable; just be sure to label each side appropriately, such as *1 of 1*, *1 of 2* or *2 of 2*.

{***NOTE****: I recognize that this idea of page-numbering may seem stupid, but you'd be surprised how many companies DON'T do this and as a result end up with frustrated Journalists on their hands.*}

Beyond the five points listed above, there are a few additional items to consider for your <u>Facts Sheets</u>

- <u>Facts Sheets</u> may or may not contain one or more graphics, such as Photos, Charts or Tables.
- <u>Facts Sheets</u> may be printed in two or more colors on an offset or digital printer.
- <u>Facts Sheets</u> must be written in a journalistic style, just as you would write a <u>News Release</u>. {*Personally, I prefer the* Associated Press *Style.*}

- The most important information must be placed at the beginning of your <u>Facts Sheets</u>, with the least important information at the end.

And if you're going to share a digital version of a <u>Facts Sheet</u> with a Journalist, I recommend you save the document first as a PDF file before sharing it.

In case you've never seen or created a <u>Facts Sheet</u> before, I've included a copy of a <u>Facts Sheet</u> on the following pages. This was something I produced for MULTIVOICE while serving as its Chief Marketing Officer.

Hopefully this example will be helpful.

66 RULES for Publicity Success

MISSION:
MULTIVOICE™ enhances the human experience by allowing people to *BE HEARD*™. We enable groups to communicate in real-time while they work or play. Hence, work becomes safer, effectiveness increases and efficiency rises, while play also becomes more playful, engaging and memorable.

OVERVIEW:
Formed in 2011, MULTIVOICE has developed mobile, hands-free wireless systems that enable secure and simultaneous group communications among fearless individuals in rigorous environments. The company's first product — the **MV-NEXUS**™ Wireless Mesh Network Intercom™ — was announced in early 2015. It allows teams of up to forty-three (43) co-workers to talk simultaneously on a secure, hands-free wireless network at distances of up to one mile apart without using a base station and can operate

- In standalone mode,
- Side-by-side with a Push-to-Talk radio network, or
- Combined with a PTT or P25 radio network.

Additionally, the MV-NEXUS allows an unlimited number of listeners on the same wireless network, while also allowing listeners to become speakers as previous speakers drop into "listen-only" mode.

INVENTIONS:
MULTIVOICE's technologies currently revolve around the Industrial, Scientific and Medical (ISM) wireless communications frequencies of 902—928MHz in a mixture of patented, patent-pending and trade secret inventions, including U.S. Patents 8,681,663 and 8,705,377. By utilizing FDMA (Frequency Division Multiple Access), TDMA (Time Division Multiple Access), Frequency-Hopping Spread Spectrum and select proprietary wireless communications methodologies, MULTIVOICE enables real-time, simultaneous, secure and hands-free audio communications among group members on a self-healing wireless network.

PRODUCTS:
Built to fit in standard *5.11-size* pockets and pouches common in military, public safety and industrial clothing and gear, MULTIVOICE's first commercially available products are the MV-NEXUS (for Industrial/Commercial use), the **MV-AUDIBLE**™ (for American football coaches), and the **MV-PROTECTOR**™ (for the Public Safety market). These products are Wireless Mesh-Network Intercoms™ that measure 5.3x3.3x1.3-inches, weigh 15.98 ounces, use two rechargeable 3000mAh Lithium-Polymer batteries, ship standard with a 3.5-inch-high antenna, and deliver up to 18 hours of actual talk time without recharging. The company's newly announced **MV-COMBINER**™ allows team members to simultaneously and securely share MV-NEXUS or MV-PROTECTOR communications across PTT, P25 and/or cellular networks. Additional MULTIVOICE accessories include a number of headset/microphone combinations, various headset cable styles and lengths, as well as detachable antennae of varying heights.

MARKETS:
MULTIVOICE's technologies represent a dramatic transformation to the way groups of individuals can safely and securely communicate simultaneously in real-time without having to use their hands. MULTIVOICE's Wireless Mesh-Network Intercoms are ideal for use today by groups in many business and government professions, including those who work in

- *Industrial/Commercial* settings,
- *Sports* (during training or games),
- *Public Safety*, and
- The *Military*.

In the consumer marketplace, we also believe that MULTIVOICE technologies will further enhance activities for families, friends and teams across a wide range of activities, including

- Snowboarding/Skiing,
- Mountain Biking,
- Road Cycling,
- Motorcycling,
- Bird-watching,
- Paintballing,
- Hunting, and
- More.

66 RULES for Publicity Success

CHANNELS:
MULTIVOICE products are currently available through a network of exclusive manufacturer representatives and affiliated dealers.

FUNDING:
MULTIVOICE received a $5.0 million round of strategic seed funding from OTTO Engineering in 2014 for a minority position in MULTIVOICE at a $25 million post-money valuation. MULTIVOICE has also raised $750,000 in "friends and family" and angel funding.

EXECUTIVES:
*Founder, President, CEO, Lead Inventor & Chairman — **Ron Fraser**:* Following a 30-plus-year career designing and developing specialized wireless communications working for Texas Instruments, TRW, the U.S. Naval Research Laboratory, the Titan Missile program, 3M and Porta Phone (among others), Ron formed MULTIVOICE in 2011.

*Co-Founder & CMO — **David Politis**:* David joined MULTIVOICE in mid-2014 following a 30-year career in technology marketing, public relations and investor relations that saw him help firms grow their valuations by over $1.1 billion. Most recently, David was CMO for Xi3 Corporation where he helped grow the company from 4 to 100 employees in 3.5 years, captured tens of thousands of hot/warms leads and identified 100s of millions of dollars in new sales opportunities.

*Co-Founder, V.P. of Product Development & Board Member — **Dustin Fraser**:* After filling executive sales and marketing positions with two technology start-ups, Dustin helped Ron launch MULTIVOICE in 2011 and was directly involved in the initial design, sourcing, marketing and sales of the MV-NEXUS and its predecessor, the MV900™.

*SVP, Business Development — **Rob Vickery**:* Rob has over 20 years of entrepreneurial and executive level sales, marketing, product development and operational experience in companies ranging from AT&T and MCI to Change.com and Pandesic (an Intel/SAP joint venture).

*Financial Advisor & Acting CFO — **Gary Reimer**:* Gary has over 30 years of senior financial experience in technology, consumer, sports and media brands, across both private and public accounting, with companies ranging from Coopers & Lybrand to HP and from Capri Sun to Real Salt Lake.

*Board Member — **Tom Schreiber**:* An Electrical Engineer by training, Tom has over 30 years of experience in a variety of start-up and multinational technology firms, with the 2nd half of his career dedicated to senior and executive management. He is the General Manager of OTTO Engineering, a position he has held since 2007.

###

MULTIVOICE, the MULTIVOICE marks and logos, *BE HEARD*, MV-NEXUS, MV-PROTECTOR, MV-AUDIBLE, Wireless Mesh-Network Intercom, and MV-COMBINER are each trademarks of MULTIVOICE. All other trademarks are property of their respective owners.

CONTACT:
David Politis, MULTIVOICE, politis@multivoice.com, 385-375-8855(w) or 801-xxx-xxxx(c)

In closing, be aware that <u>Facts Sheets</u> can be considered expanded versions of a Written Elevator Pitch — whether they are written about a company, product, service, person or invention (as described back in RULE #4).

As such, after producing your first <u>Facts Sheet</u>, you should have a one-page document you can share with Journalists and others that provides

> *an easy-to-understand overview of a company, product, service, invention or person.*

And if not, keep massaging, editing and refining until you get it just right.

> {**NOTE**: *Although a <u>Biography</u> and a <u>Facts Sheet</u> about the same person can contain much of the same information, their purposes and formats are definitely different — hence, the inclusion of <u>Facts Sheets</u> within this RULE and the separate RULE #14 about <u>Biographies</u> later in this book.*}

= = = = = = = = = = = = = = = = = = = =

RULE #13: <u>**Backgrounders**</u> are *Must Haves*

If <u>Facts Sheets</u> are described in the previous RULE as
"***expanded*** *versions of a Written Elevator Pitch,*" then
<u>Backgrounders</u> can be considered as **detailed** versions of a
Written Elevator Pitch.

Hence, a <u>Backgrounder</u> is a

> *Multipage document that provides a detailed overview of a*
> *company, product(s), service(s), invention(s) or person/people.*

So . . . while <u>Facts Sheets</u> limit the writer to one single sheet of
paper (single- or double-sided), <u>Backgrounders</u> have no such
limitation. In fact, I've seen <u>Company Backgrounders</u> as long
as 12 pages in length and as short as four pages.

The critical distinction between these two Publicity tools is this:

- <u>Facts Sheets</u> contain **condensed information**, while
- <u>Backgrounders</u> contain **detailed information**.

What's the difference between **condensed** and **detailed**?
That's for you to decide.

But if your company, product(s), service(s), invention(s) and/or
people (or an individual person) warrants a <u>Backgrounder</u>, then
have at it.

Much like <u>Facts Sheets</u>, I believe that <u>Backgrounders</u> must also
include the following five items:

1. **A Title, Headline and/or Logo** (to clarify
   who/what this <u>Backgrounder</u> is about),

2. **Publication Date** (to notify the reader as to how current the information is in that specific Backgrounder),
3. **Subheads** (to make it easier for a Journalist to scan for the information he/she is most interested in reading),
4. **24x7x365 Contact Info**, and
5. **Page Numbers**.

Beyond the five points listed above, there are a few additional items to consider for your Backgrounders:

- Backgrounders typically DO contain one or more graphics, such as Photos, Charts or Tables.
- Backgrounders may also be printed in two or more colors on an offset or digital printer, just as you can with Facts Sheets.
- Backgrounders must also be written in a journalistic style, just as you would write a News Release or Facts Sheet. {*Here again, I prefer to use the* Associated Press *Style.*}
- The most important information must be placed at the beginning of your Backgrounders, with the least important information at the end.

And if you're going to share a digital version of a Backgrounder with a Journalist, I recommend you save the file first as a PDF file before passing it along.

= =

RULE #14: <u>Biographies</u> are *Must Haves*

Even if your company only has one person working for it —
YOU — your company should still have <u>Biographies</u> created
about *you*. And I do mean <u>Biographies</u>, as in more than one.
But more about that later.

If your company has more than one person working for it, then
you need to decide how many of those people need to have a
professional <u>Biography</u> written about them to support your
Publicity efforts.

For example, the larger the company, the fewer employees
(percentage-wise) who need to have <u>Biographies</u> created and
published for them — such as the most senior executives,
especially C-Level execs like Chief Executive Officers (CEOs),
Chief Operations Officers (COOs), Chief Financial Officers
(CFOs), Chief Marketing Officers (CMOs), etc. Conversely,
I've seen some firms with fewer than 50 employees include
<u>Biographies</u> for every single employee on the company's
Websites. In the end, this will be your decision.

If you're going to use <u>Biographies</u> as part of your Publicity
efforts, then you'll need to write them in a journalistic format.
{*Again, I recommend following the* Associated Press *Style.*}

When it comes to <u>Biographies</u>, I believe you will need three
versions for each person "worthy" of a bio at your firm. These
are

1. A <u>50-Word Biography</u>,
2. A <u>200-word Biography</u>, and
3. A *LinkedIn* Profile.

Let's consider each in order.

The 50-Word Biography

In many ways, the 50-Word Biography is much like the Written Elevator Pitch. And in that regard, the 50-Word Biography is arguably the hardest Biography to write because you have to decide what few bits of information should be included versus those to be left out.

To be clear, if you end up with a few words more or less than 50 words when writing a 50-Word Biography, that's fine. The idea is to be in the ballpark from a word count standpoint.

The 200-Word Biography

Just as Facts Sheets are designed to provide Journalists with "a quick way to get up-to-speed" on a topic, a 200-Word Biography does the exact same thing for an individual.

In the same way that a Facts Sheet provides a **condensed** viewpoint of what is included in a Written Elevator Pitch, a 200-Word Biography conversely provides **expanded** information versus what is found in a 50-Word Biography.

And as with the 50-Word Biography, if you end up with a few words more or less than 200 words when writing a 200-Word Biography, that's fine. The idea is to be close to 200 words.

The *LinkedIn* Profile

As of early 2016, there are more than 400 million people around the globe with a Profile on *LinkedIn*. In roughly a dozen years, it has become ***THE*** professional Social Media platform for business professionals around the world, with versions currently published in over 20 languages.

While addressing a class of Communications students at a university recently, I told them that they were crazy if they did not have a *LinkedIn* Profile. Thankfully, nearly all of them had already gotten the message from their professors.

Shockingly, there are still a fairly high number of business professionals who do not believe that *LinkedIn* is important to them. Why do I believe this? Because

- They do not have a *LinkedIn* Profile at all, or because
- Their *LinkedIn* Profile is seriously incomplete.

And in some regards, having a cursory or seriously incomplete *LinkedIn* Profile is worse than not having a *LinkedIn* Profile at all.

At a minimum, you should consider your *LinkedIn* Profile as an augmentation to your Biography or professional resumé. At best, your *LinkedIn* Profile will become the equivalent of *a living, breathing Marketing piece* for you that can be used to passively or actively reach millions of prospective customers, partners, investors, employees, and yes, Journalists (and more) everywhere *LinkedIn* is in use — which is a lot of places.

I won't spend a lot of space here diving into the minutiae of what you should or shouldn't include in a *LinkedIn* Profile, especially since a *Google* search taken moments ago generated over 19 million hits for the phrase "What should I include in my *LinkedIn* Profile?"

However, I will provide you with a few suggestions of what I feel are *the minimum crucial pieces of content* for each *LinkedIn* Profile — at least those profiles worth their salt.

1. Ideally, use a **Professionally taken Photograph** for your Profile Photo. (If you don't have a Photo taken by

a professional Photographer already in your possession, consider getting one. The expense is worth it. Upload a closely cropped Photo of your head or head and shoulders, typically known as a headshot. Understand that frequent *LinkedIn* users automatically discount Profiles without Photos, as well as those that use unprofessional Photos.)

2. **List your Current Position** and **at LEAST two previous positions**. (Understand that you don't have to list all of your professional positions. But headhunters and executive recruiters will tell you that individuals who only list one position are not taken seriously. With each position, be sure to include enough relevant information to provide readers with a good overview of your accomplishments and responsibilities.)

3. At a minimum, **List the Last School you Attended or Graduated from**, as well as the degree or certificate you obtained (or were pursuing). Hopefully this is self-explanatory. But if not, at a minimum it will help fellow alumni to find you on *LinkedIn*. And no, you do NOT need to include the year you graduated or were awarded a certificate. The decision of whether or not to do so is left up to you.

4. **Upload a Background Image**. (This is the image found at the very top of each *LinkedIn* Profile behind your Photo and employment/educational summary. Here again, heavy *LinkedIn* users do not take *LinkedIn* Profiles seriously if they do not have a Background Image.)

5. The **Professional Summary** of your *LinkedIn* Profile will be crucial to your success on this Social Media platform; the Summary can also greatly assist you with your Publicity program. (Be aware that nearly all of *LinkedIn* has limitations on the amount of space you can use for each section, and your Professional Summary is

no exception. The limit here is 2,000 characters. Thankfully, the *LinkedIn* platform keeps track of your character use IF you are writing your Professional Summary within *LinkedIn*. However, I do NOT recommend this. Rather, I recommend you write your Professional Summary in your favorite word processor and keep track of your character count there. This will allow you to also use the spellchecker of your word processor, a feature LinkedIn does not have.)

6. **Volunteer Experience**, especially as it relates to your career, is also an important component to include in your *LinkedIn* Profile. (Community service is also good to include in this section of your *LinkedIn* Profile as it shows well-roundedness. For example, I have included information about my work as a youth sports coach, my volunteer service with the Boy Scouts of America, and my work as a board member for the Utah chapter of NAMI — the National Association for the Mentally Ill — within this section of my *LinkedIn* Profile.)

7. If you speak a foreign **Language**, you should include this in your *LinkedIn* Profile too. (Being able to communicate in two or more languages is actually a pretty big deal, so if you can, you should include this in your *LinkedIn* Profile. And if you're a computer programmer, I could probably be convinced that you can/should include computer languages in this section — but ONLY if you're truly proficient in said language/languages and ONLY if that computer language is still prominently in use today. Case in point, the fact that I took classes in MS-DOS and the Basic programming language back when I was in college doesn't count.)

8. Last but not least, you HAVE TO include **Contact Info** within your *LinkedIn* Profile. (At a minimum, this should be your email address, which means that if you're a business owner, this should be your work email

address, but you can also include your personal email address as well. You also need to be aware that what all *LinkedIn* users see of your *LinkedIn* **Contact Info** is different than what your Connections can see.)

By way of comparison, if Backgrounders are designed to provide a **detailed** overview about companies, products, services, inventions or people, *LinkedIn* Profiles do the exact same thing — but within this Social Media platform instead.

As a result, I feel that if people begin by completing these eight recommended sections of their *LinkedIn* Profiles, they will be well on their way to becoming what are known as "*LinkedIn* All-Stars."

= =

RULE #15: Use <u>White Papers</u>, <u>Position Papers</u>, and <u>Industry Overviews</u> when You Need an Authoritative, yet Impartial, Platform

If you are faced with the challenge of addressing a complex topic or issue, chances are it is time to turn to one of several similar PR/Marketing tools, each of which can provide an authoritative, yet impartial, voice that can swing the tide in your favor. The approaches I'm referring to are <u>White Papers</u>, <u>Position Papers</u> and <u>Industry Overviews</u>.

CASE STUDY: AMC's Industry Overview

A few years after leaving college, I was working with Applied Microsystems Corporation, a Washington-based company that was about to disrupt the way companies developed new products that featured microprocessors embedded inside them.

Up until that point, each microprocessor manufacturer had its own Microprocessor Development System. Each MDS was literally a single-purpose engineering workstation customized specifically to work on a particular microprocessor, yet would be operated side-by-side with an engineer's primary computer/workstation at his desk or workbench. In other words, it was a highly inefficient setup. And each of the primary manufacturers played this game: Intel, Motorola, Hewlett Packard, and others.

Into this world swooped AMC with the newfangled idea that engineers didn't need a separate machine beyond their current workstation. Rather, AMC proposed a new type of device that could leverage the capabilities of the existing machines engineers already used, something AMC called In-Circuit Emulators.

The goal at our PR/Advertising agency was to help AMC overcome the industry inertia behind the MDS approach to

56

microprocessor development and to consider an in-circuit emulation process — one that would be both faster and less expensive than the traditional methodology.

Central to our strategy was the creation and dissemination of an <u>Industry Overview</u> that highlighted

- *The history of microprocessor development, and*
- *The current state of microprocessor development.*

The <u>Industry Overview</u> then made the case for a new approach to microprocessor development using

- *Existing workstations/computers,*
- *New high-speed communications capabilities of such machines, namely SCSI ports, and then it specifically outlined*
- *The capabilities of In-Circuit Emulators from AMC.*

By the time I finished writing AMC's <u>Industry Overview on Microprocessor Development Systems</u>, it was 10 single-sided pages long, including a few graphics. To percolate this transformative concept into the engineering community, we selectively targeted key Reporters and Editors for a bi-coastal press tour at 10 industry magazines, ranging from Computer Design to EE Times.

Within four months, eight of the 10 publications had covered AMC's breakthrough development hypothesis, with three of the magazines publishing a copy of one or more of the illustrations we used to show that AMC's predicted industry shift was about to occur. More importantly, within two years, five of the six leading microprocessor manufacturers had abandoned MDS systems altogether in favor of In-Circuit Emulators. Additionally, AMC grew from $10 million to $40 million in annual revenue during *the same time frame — all on the back of its new In-Circuit Emulator business.*

Perhaps more instructive, however, is that we did NOT take any products or product information with us on this <u>Industry Overview</u> Press Tour. In fact, AMC did not announce the release of its first In-Circuit Emulators until several months after the Press Tour.

In simplistic terms, <u>Industry Overviews</u>, <u>Position Papers</u> and <u>White Papers</u> are each designed to allow organizations to present their side of a complex topic or issue in an authoritative manner. The hope is that by taking this path, organizations can educate and/or persuade targeted individuals to new ways of thinking and/or acting and thereby achieve favorable outcomes.

Ideally, regardless of the vehicle chosen, <u>Position Papers</u>, <u>Industry Overviews</u> and <u>White Papers</u> are written from an impartial viewpoint. In fact, the more impartial the better as this approach will dramatically increase the odds of persuading others to your point of view.

From a logistical standpoint, I have seen <u>White Papers</u> and <u>Industry Overviews</u> as short as six pages in length and as long as 20 pages. Conversely, a <u>Position Paper</u> can be 20 pages or longer; in its simplest form, though, a Position Paper can be as simple as a <u>Letter to the Editor</u> (or a published Column).

According to *Wikipedia* (as of 12-27-15), a <u>White Paper</u> is

> *". . . an authoritative report or guide that informs readers concisely about a complex issue and presents the issuing body's philosophy on the matter. It is meant to help readers understand an issue, solve a problem, or make a decision."*

On the other hand, *Wikipedia* defines a <u>Position Paper</u> thusly:

". . . an essay that presents an opinion about an issue, typically that of the author or another specified entity, such as a political party. Position papers are published in academia, in politics, in law and other domains. Position papers range from the simplest format of a Letter to the Editor through to the most complex in the form of an academic position paper. Position papers are also used by large organizations to make public the official beliefs and recommendations of the group."

In contrast, *WiseGeek.com* states that an <u>Industry Overview</u>

". . . usually defines the industry, talks about its major products, and discusses the size. It can include a list of major companies and provide information about the number of people working in the industry, baseline qualifications needed to enter various job positions, and the earnings of the industry in recent years. Graphs and Charts may offer visual representations of data, showing people how earnings, size, and other key metrics change over time."

Unlike the world I faced in the mid-1990s where traditional media outlets were virtually the only way organizations could reach large numbers of individuals all at once, this is no longer the case (due to the widespread use of the World Wide Web). Hence, although I still believe there can be great value in engaging with targeted Journalists, Analysts and other influencers on complex topics that impact your company and/or industry, I am also convinced in the value of direct contact between organizations and their targeted publics.

And yes, such a strategy includes using <u>Industry Overviews</u>, <u>Position Papers</u> and <u>White Papers</u> — especially when it comes to addressing complex issues.

= =

RULE #16: Use the Right Photos

Every picture tells a story, don't it?

This line, penned by British Rockers Ron Wood and Rod Stewart and taken from the 1971 Stewart album and song, Every Picture Tells A Story, was described by AllMusic's Denise Sullivan as "defining rock & roll."

Not only does this phrase capture the essence of early 1970s "rock & roll," but it also stands in great harmony with the following statement from over 100 years ago:

"A picture is worth a thousand words."

For better or worse, crafting/using the right Photo will often mean the difference between ***Publicity Success*** and failure.

Theoretically, I could spend an entire book just addressing the nuances of Photography, the elements that make up a good Photo versus a great one, as well as some of the ways to use Photography in today's Marketing world. However, that is not the purpose of 66 RULES for Publicity Success, nor is this the right venue for such an examination.

However, it ***is*** appropriate to describe three Photograph topics that you will need to understand for your Publicity campaigns, namely **Taking Photographs**, **Photo Types** and **Legal Considerations**.

- Unfortunately, many people believe they are experts at **Taking Photographs**, especially since anyone with a smartphone also has in their hands a pretty awesome digital camera. The reality is that nothing could be further from the truth, especially when it comes to professional-quality Photos. Not that Photos taken with a smartphone don't have their place, because they do.

However, I believe that the sooner firms can utilize a professional Photographer, the better off they will be and the better their Photos will look. If/when you engage a professional Photographer, be sure that you do **_NOT_** hand off the responsibility for overseeing and directing the Photography process to the Photographer — this responsibility falls to you.

- There are five main **Photo Types** used for Publicity and Marketing purposes — Product Photos, Service Photos, Personnel Photos, Social Media Photos and Emotion Photos.
    - Product Photos can be "beauty shots" (pictures where the product is the only item included in the Photograph) or "in-use shots" (Photos that show a product being used by one person or a group of people).
    - Service Photos are designed to communicate the type and value of a service delivered by an organization.
    - Personnel Photos are either "headshots" (close-up Photos of a person's head or head/shoulders) or "active shots" that show the individual doing something.
    - Social Media Photos are typically images shot with smartphones published via Social Media platforms.
    - Emotion Photos are images that invoke an emotion or feeling in the viewer, even if the Photo has nothing to do with a particular organization per se.

- Primary Photography **Legal Considerations** revolve around two issues: <u>Model Releases</u> and <u>Usage Rights</u>:
  - o If you use anyone else in a Photograph beside yourself (and that Photo is used for commercial purposes), then you must have the permission of that individual to use her/his image (via a <u>Model Release</u> form), and
  - o You must also pay such individuals some form of <u>Consideration</u> for the use of their image. You can pay them in one of two ways: with money or with some other agreed upon form of compensation that has recognized value, such as a car, a meal, ski tickets, etc.
  - o If you use a professional Photographer, whether this person is an independent or on your staff, that individual actually owns the Photographs she/he shoots for you. Ergo, you need to agree in advance to what are known as <u>Usage Rights</u>. My recommendation is that you always buy *Unlimited, Royalty-Free Usage Rights.*

I recommend looking for free examples of Model Release forms on the Internet. You can also find additional information about Photography Usage Rights by searching on the 'Net.

In most instances, I believe you should save Photographs in the JPEG format at a resolution of 300dpi (dots per inch) or higher. Occasionally, you may need to save Photos in the PNG format (commonly used on the Web) or in a TIFF format, typically very high-resolution images often used by Graphic Designers and Art Directors.

= =

RULE #17: Select Other Graphics to Tell Your Story

Sometimes there is really no way a Photograph can be shot or captured so that it will communicate everything necessary in one image. In these instances, there are five other types of graphics that can be used in place of a Photo:

- **Charts**,
- **Tables**,
- **Graphs**,
- **Illustrations**, and
- **CG Images**.

I suspect most readers will understand what **Charts**, **Tables** and **Graphs** are, so I won't take time here to describe them or their usage.

Illustrations are a different animal altogether, but they too have a definite place in this list of Other Graphics. For example, I've had a number of medical and scientific clients during my career that successfully used **Illustrations** to help them communicate quickly and clearly with their targeted audiences. Additionally, I have seen other companies turn to comic-book-style Illustrations to help them communicate or drive home a message as part of their PR or Marketing programs. Either way, unless you have professional training or a personal background as an Illustrator, you'll most likely need to select and hire a professional to create your **Illustrations**.

Conversely, **CG Images** are Computer- or Web-Generated Images; by using this type of graphic one can create simple to elaborate images, illustrations, objects and more. These can include finished **CG Images** that incorporate words to help better explain your product, service or concept via callouts, descriptions or captions. Another form of **CG Image** is a <u>Photo Composition</u> where two or more Photos are combined into one finished Photo.

{***NOTE****: Professional Artists, Painters, Illustrators, Graphic Designers and Art Directors (digital or traditional) are each granted the same ownership rights for any item they create. In the eyes of the U.S. judicial system, this puts them in the same classification as Photographers, meaning they own their creative works and NOT you — unless, that is, you buy Usage Rights or the piece was created for you via contract as a Hired Work or as Work-for-Hire. To be clear, I am not an attorney, so I am only sharing my business experience with you and not offering legal advice here.*

So . . . please be sure to visit first with an attorney with specific understanding about the ownership of creative works before you hire your first Photographer, Artist, Painter, Illustrator, Graphic Designer and/or Art Director. }

= = = = = = = = = = = = = = = = = = =

RULE #18: Provide 24x7x365 Contact Info — Always

If you work in public relations and do NOT include some form of **around-the-clock contact information** on every PR document you distribute to Journalists, you are nuts.

What am I talking about? Just about anything, such as:

- Press Releases,
- News Briefs,
- Media Alerts,
- Facts Sheets,
- FAQs,
- Q&As,
- White Papers,
- Industry Overviews,
- Biographies,
- Photos,
- Infographics,
- Business Cards,
- Websites,
- Etc., etc., etc.

If a Journalist is on a deadline and she cannot reach you to get that one bit of information needed for her story, you're toast. Chances are that Journalist will delete your company's info from the story, curse your name, and move on to someone else.

Always include **24x7 Contact Information** on EVERY digital and physical PR piece you produce and distribute.

= = = = = = = = = = = = = = = = = = = =

BONUS RULE: Create a Simple Visual to Showcase Your Positioning & Messaging

Although the phrase "A picture is worth a thousand words" is obviously a cliché, the reality is that it is often much easier (and faster) to communicate an idea via a picture or other visual image.

I believe this concept is especially true when it comes to communicating the Positioning and Messaging of a product, service or company relative to its peers or competitors.

So . . . whether you use a Graph, Chart, Table, Diagram, Infographic or some other visual mechanism, I strongly urge you to create a one-page (or smaller), simple-to-comprehend visual that can be used to showcase the Positioning/Messaging of your product, service or company relative to its peers or competitors.

= = = = = = = = = = = = = = = = = = = =

BONUS RULE: *Record a Short Video to Help Visually and Audibly Showcase Your Positioning and Messaging*

Some people learn by doing, others by reading, still others by listening. And because some people learn best by listening, I believe you should also seriously consider making a short recording to help explain your Positioning and Messaging.

Although you're probably thinking that I meant an audio recording, I did not. The reality is that you'll actually get better engagement if you make and publish a video recording, both from individuals who are audible learners, as well as those who are visual learners.

Besides, once you have a video recording in place, it's a relatively simple process to extract the audio track so you can have that too (should you need it).

= = = = = = = = = = = = = = = = = = = =

SECTION 4: "STOP THE PRESSES"

By now you hopefully have a much better handle on the skills of Positioning and Messaging, while also gaining a greater understanding of two key publics: Journalists and Customers (both current and prospective).

In addition, I've hopefully helped you understand some of the most widely used vehicles for capturing key background information and delivering it to all of your various target-audience members, but particularly when you do so with Journalists.

Now it's time to learn the best ways to craft and deliver newsworthy information to members of the media, while also learning how to do so in ways that will help you have the greatest likelihood of producing the results you want — ***Publicity Success***.

So in this ***"STOP THE PRESSES"*** section, I focus on two primary areas:

- News Releases, and
- Pitching the Media.

And *yes*, even though we now live in a hyper-connected world that (at times) seems to move at the speed of light, the reality is that properly produced News Releases are still the best way to encapsulate new news and data for Journalists. In fact, even if a News Release is never distributed beyond an audience of one solitary person, such documents are still the best way for your business to communicate out to the world.

This being the case, it is also true that some of your best Publicity efforts will come through highly targeted pitches: those times when you package-up a story specifically for one market, one media outlet, or, more likely, one individual Journalist.

So here we go. It's time to learn how you can get an Editor to yell, ***"STOP THE PRESSES."***

= = = = = = = = = = = = = = = = = = = =

RULE #19: News Releases Still Matter

With apologies in advance to the memory of Francis Pharcellus Church (long-time Journalist and author of the world-famous "Yes, Virginia, There is a Santa Claus" editorial that ran in the *New York Sun* on September 21, 1897), I emphatically state that

"Yes, News Releases still matter."

I believe releases matter for several reasons, but for this book, let me name five reasons.

- News Releases still give companies control over their Messaging. The ability of organizations to distribute news and information directly to clients, partners, investors, suppliers and others via email, Websites, Blogs, Social Media and more gives PR and Marketing professionals the ability to bypass the gatekeeping function of the media.

- Some media outlets and Bloggers will re-publish News Releases in full or in part. This ensures that all or some of a company's announcements will reach selected/targeted audience members in at least some type of their intended form/language.

- Short-handed news staffs have less time to do more work than ever before. In this environment, well-written News Releases provide valuable sources of information for news outlets and their Journalists. And in some instances, releases can be published verbatim by targeted news outlets, including those that would have never done so in the past, including *Bloomberg*, *Marketwatch*, *Reuters*, and *The Wall Street Journal*, just to name a few.

- For publicly traded companies, News Releases are almost always a must. In fact, official News Releases are one of only a handful of methods accepted by the U.S. Securities and Exchange Commission for full-disclosure of what is termed by the SEC as "material" and "non-public" news/information.

- Digital media equals nearly instantaneous, worldwide distribution for your news. Here's what I mean. Craft a News Release and then
    o Distribute it via a Commercial Wire Service;
    o Upload it to your Website;
    o Reference it on your Blog;
    o Shoot it out to Journalists, Analysts and Bloggers via email;
    o Share it with customers, partners, investors, employees and others via email;
    o Post it on your *Facebook* Wall;
    o Tweet about it on *Twitter*;
    o Describe the highlights in a short *YouTube* video;
    o Highlight it via a text message or SMS feed;
    o Highlight it via a *LinkedIn* Update;
    o Pin it on your *Pinterest* Page;
    o Etc., etc., etc.

In other words, with a little bit of forethought and advance legwork, you can reach millions of current or prospective customers, partners, investors, employees, Journalists, Analysts and/or influencers with your news announcement all within a matter of minutes.

There are other reasons why I believe News Releases are still crucial in the PR world, but I suspect these will suffice for now.

= =

RULE #20: "A," "B" and "C" News Releases

Be honest with yourself: Not everything that happens at your company (or to your client) is newsworthy — *certainly not to every Reporter or media outlet* — regardless of what you may think {*or what your boss or client thinks, for that matter*}.

Nevertheless, I'd bet that something newsworthy is happening nearly each and every week at your company.

The challenge is to

- *Set proper expectations* internally, and
- Target *the right news to the best news organization* and/or Journalist.

One way to do this is through a *Ranking System* for your <u>News Releases</u>. For example, I classify press releases as being an "A," "B" or "C" <u>News Release</u>, and I do this by making a judgment call on every bit of prospective news I uncover inside client organizations.

For example, "A" <u>News Releases</u> contain news or information that I believe has the prospect of being translated into a top story, one that will

- Lead the top of a newscast,
- Be the No. 1 story in a particular section of a newspaper or magazine, or
- Get picked up by a Wire Service, syndicator or online news aggregator.

One example of an "A" <u>News Release</u> I worked on was the news that Schwinn Bicycles was launching the fastest re-charging electric bicycle on the planet. Due to increased sensitivities about environmental concerns, this news had far-reaching implications across the United States, making it an "A" release for many mass market media outlets.

Another example of an "A" News Release was the announcement from Coherex Medical that it had received CE Mark Clearance for its Coherex FlatStent EF PFO Closure System. From my perspective, this announcement warranted "A" status because millions of people have clogged blood vessels, and the Coherex device helped alleviate complications that could arise during surgeries to repair such blockages.

By contrast, "B" <u>News Releases</u> contain news or information I believe has the prospect of being used in a solid story, one that might

- Warrant a standalone story in a particular section of a newspaper or magazine,
- Be included in a larger story, perhaps a trend piece (online, in print or in a broadcast venue),
- Be mentioned in a newscast, or
- Generate coverage in specialized media outlets or Blogs.

For example, the closing of a multi-million-dollar round of venture capital funding probably qualifies as a solid "B" news release.

Although still newsworthy, "C" <u>News Releases</u> truly have limited focus and/or news appeal.

Examples of "C" <u>News Releases</u> include most

- New hires or promotions,
- Moves to a new location or expanding office space,

- Smaller charitable donations or activities,
- Etc.

In other words, they're still newsworthy announcements; it's just that the probable impact of such news is limited in scope.

Which brings me back to the first three points made at the beginning of this RULE:

- Be honest with yourself about the particular newsworthiness of any given event, news or piece of info.
- Make sure others share your honest appraisal (i.e., set proper expectations).
- Target the right news to the right Journalist and/or media outlet.

If you take this approach to <u>News Releases</u>, chances are you'll have a lot more ***Publicity Success*** (and less heartburn in the process).

= = = = = = = = = = = = = = = = = = = =

RULE #21: Write Short Headlines

Shorter headlines are harder to write than long headlines. I get it.

Nevertheless, *short headlines are typically better than long headlines.*

This works for <u>News Releases</u>, email subject lines, articles, columns, ads, brochures . . . just about anything that needs a headline.

Yes, it's harder to do. But they're easier to read. And search engines like *Google* LOVE short headlines. *(Just ask any of your friends in Search Engine Optimization or Marketing.)*

RULE of thumb:

<u>Write short headlines</u>.

{NOTE: As of this writing, the general consensus is that headlines of less than 70 characters are ideal, including spaces between words and punctuation. To see the latest thoughts about this, conduct an Internet search for the phrase "short headlines" + SEO and see what burbles to the top of your search.}

= = = = = = = = = = = = = = = = = = = =

RULE #22: Sometimes You Have to Write a Really, Really Long Headline

Maybe it's your boss's fault . . . or your client's fault. *(Then again, it's probably your fault, since you're the one calling the shots.)*

But for some reason you've got to squeeze two company names and a product name and some adjectives and adverbs all into one little ol' headline. Okay, that happens sometimes.

However, shorter headlines are still better. So if you can, try to pare words (and character counts) where possible.

Another way to approach this task is to **use a shorter headline that is supported by a subhead**, even a lengthy one.

However, if you absolutely, positively cannot convince all involved to go with a shorter headline, don't sweat it (this time at least). Fight the battle on the next go-round.

= = = = = = = = = = = = = = = = = = = =

BONUS RULE: Understanding the "Journalist Mindset"

As mentioned earlier in this book, I studied Mass Communications at BYU, with a special emphasis in the area of Public Relations.

Back in the day, a PR student at BYU could not graduate unless she/he took at least two Journalism courses: one, an Introductory course in Reporting, and a second class where you were required to work as a Staff Reporter for the on-campus student newspaper, known then as The Daily Universe.

As luck would have it, the timing worked out so that I took my Staff Reporting class during an 8-week Summer Term and not during a traditional 16-week-long Fall or Winter Semester. In other words, on the surface, I didn't have a lot of calendar time to generate a number of portfolio-worthy pieces that Summer Term, which was a bit concerning to me.

Then again, what was even more disconcerting was what a fellow PR student told me my first day at The Daily Universe. *It was her last day there, and I was slated to take over her Beat: the Engineering and Science Departments on campus. In her words, it was a dreadful assignment as she had not been able to produce a single story through either Department during the preceding Spring Term.*

And yet, in less than a week at The Daily Universe, *I uncovered two significant stories from these Departments, one of which involved a multimillion-dollar grant from IBM to the Engineering Department. Turns out both of these stories had been figuratively "sitting there" for the entire preceding Term merely waiting to be uncovered and reported to the BYU world.*

So was I lucky and she unlucky? Perhaps.

However, what I believe is more likely is that I was able to think and act like a Journalist more than she was. In fact, I would propose that I became an actual Journalist (at least for that Summer Term, many years ago), and that, my friend, is the purpose of this BONUS RULE.

In other words, **you HAVE TO be able to think (and act) like a Journalist to be truly successful in your Publicity efforts.**

At its core, this means that as a business owner you need to be completely honest with yourself when evaluating the newsworthiness of what it is you have done, are doing or plan to do. In other words, you need to be able to ascertain the value of any announcement you want to make against a backdrop of your answer to the following question:

"Who will care about this — and why?"

The more that you can learn to become (No — to **BE***) absolutely objective in your Publicity endeavors, the less likely you will be to spin your wheels pursuing so-called big announcements that no one really cares about . . . especially Journalists.*

And, in truth, the more that you can learn to adapt to a Journalist Mindset, the greater the likelihood that Journalists will come to respect and trust you, especially when you say, "I think I've got a story for you."

That's why when I called the student Editor at The Daily Universe *during the next Fall Semester and told him I had a story that needed to be on the front page the following morning —* my own version of yelling "STOP THE PRESSES" *— he gave me the courtesy of letting me, a non-journalism student, explain what I had uncovered. And that's also why the next morning my bylined story about the arrest of a bank robbery suspect found hiding inside a BYU student's apartment landed on the front page of the* Universe, *scooping every other media outlet in the state.*

That, I believe, is what it means to

Understand the "Journalist Mindset."

= = = = = = = = = = = = = = = = = = = =

RULE #23: Find the Best Media Outlet

Historically, a lot of PR professionals have used the "spray and pray" approach to media relations, which is just a fancy way of saying they would send out one <u>News Release</u> to as many Journalists as possible all at the same time. That's kind of like being a duck hunter who uses a machine gun when going hunting.

In other words . . . *just pull the trigger and hope you knock something out of the sky.*

To be honest, there are times when blasting out a release to lots of Journalists at the same time is the best tactic. And in some instances (such as with publicly traded companies), you may be legally obligated to disseminate news to numerous media outlets/Journalists all at the same time.

However, when it comes to story pitching and placement, you will typically be better off if you figure out one specific media outlet to target instead of many. So how do you do that?

The key issue here is focus. You should always be able to answer a series of basic questions designed to help you focus your thinking, questions such as:

- What's the story idea about?
- Who will find it most interesting?
  - o Consumers?
  - o Engineers?
  - o Quilters?
  - o Political junkies?
  - o Someone else?
- And why?

And then you should ask yourself, "Can the focus of the story idea be tightened even more?"

For example, you may be working for Berkeley (the fishing products company) and be planning the launch of a new product.

Depending upon the specifics of the new product, however, you might successfully pitch and land stories

- On TV,
- On radio,
- On Blogs,
- In newspapers,
- In outdoor magazines,
- In fishing magazines, and
- In fly fishing magazines (just to name a few).

To do this successfully, you should make sure you

- *Analyze the various categories of media outlets,* and
- *Target the outlets you're most likely to have success with* (based upon your pitch).

= = = = = = = = = = = = = = = = = = = =

RULE #24: Match Your Story Idea to the Right Journalist

Finding the right media outlet is only part of the job. You also need to make sure you **focus your pitch on the right Journalist** (or Producer) for the story.

For example, if you're going to run a story idea by Jasen Lee of the *Deseret News*, you'll have a better chance for success if you have a business angle for your pitch.

Conversely, if you're working on a consumer tech story for *The Wall Street Journal*, Joanna Stern is definitely your best bet.

Bottom line for your best results? Find the right Journalist for the story.

= = = = = = = = = = = = = = = = = = = =

RULE #25: Think Visually When You Pitch

In Rule #16, and in a prior BONUS RULE, I mentioned the following cliché:

"A picture is worth a thousand words."

But just because it's a cliché doesn't mean the statement is false. And when it comes to media relations, having artwork to augment your Publicity efforts can dramatically increase your chance for success.

So whether you're pitching a story idea to a Journalist or crafting your next <u>News Release</u>, one way to increase your chances for media coverage success is to *think visually*.

What I mean by "think visually" is to consider what artwork could be used with your story, whether it's

- Still Photography,
- Video footage, or
- Some form of 2-D graphic (like a pie Chart or Graph).

For example, several years ago a couple of cyclists got the brilliant idea to combine cycling with unique Halloween costumes to help communicate the idea that bicyclists and cars need to share the road.

In concept, this media relations idea was quite simple. But by donning inflatable sumo wrestler suits on Halloween Day and riding along major thoroughfares on their road bikes throughout their metropolitan area, these cyclists were able to attract significant visibility for their cause, both in print and on TV.

All because a couple of guys put their heads together and came up with a very visual way to help communicate their message.

In reality, this RULE is deployed countless times each day by savvy PR pros around the world. So *think visually* to maximize your ***Publicity Success***.

= = = = = = = = = = = = = = = = = = = =

RULE #26: Use the Phone

In today's hyper-connected world, what with email, *Twitter* accounts, *Facebook* Pages, *LinkedIn* Profiles and other Social Media and social networking sites/services being used numerous times each day by nearly everyone in the developed world, it's easy to get all caught-up in developing a digital-only approach to working with Journalists.

Sometimes, however, the best thing to do is to pick up the stupid phone and call a Reporter.

To be clear, this is not something I recommend all of the time. But **on occasion**, making a phone call is the easiest (and fastest) way to connect with a Journalist and communicate exactly what you need to communicate.

= =

RULE #27: Ask, "Are You On Deadline?"

When you call Journalists (after introducing yourself and who you represent), the first words out of your mouth need to be

"Are you on deadline?"

The truth of the matter is that Journalists are always on deadline, but even more so in today's hyper-connected, always-on world.

Not being courteous enough to utter those four simple words — ***Are you on deadline?*** — merely illustrates how little you understand the inner workings of a newsroom.

Whether you are contacting a freelancer, the *Chicago Tribune* or a Blogger organization, the question still stands:

"Are you on deadline?"

= = = = = = = = = = = = = = = = = = = =

BONUS RULE: *Pitch a <u>Trend</u> Story*

If you seem to be running into difficulties getting Journalists to "bite" on your story pitches, consider pitching a <u>Trend Story</u> the next time around.

In simplest terms this means you need to figure out one way that you, your company and/or products/services are part of a larger, overall trend — specifically, a new trend.

Ideally, you will be able to offer the Journalist examples of how this trend affects a growing and/or large segment of the population. And you will also be able to suggest names of competitors, industry experts and other sources to the Journalist that will make his/her task easier in producing this <u>Trend Story</u>.

I've used this tactic several times throughout my career and, without exception, the idea for each <u>Trend Story</u> was well received.

A prime example of this is described in the "Milking the Spider" CASE STUDY found in the pages ahead. Although I won't go into all the details here, I will say this particular <u>Trend Story</u> was critical to the future **Publicity Success** *for Natural Product Sciences.*

= =

RULE #28: Tweak the Story Angle

What happens if you've identified the right category of media outlets for your story idea, but can't decide which specific media outlet to pitch?

Simple. Tweak your pitch to come up with more than one slant to the story.

For instance, going back to the idea found in RULE #23, let's say Berkeley is coming out with a new line of fishing hooks. And for argument's sake, let's say these new hooks are made out of titanium.

In this example, chances are Berkeley would launch packages of snelled hooks (hooks that are sold in small packages and are pre-tied onto short leaders so they're easy to attach and detach from one's fishing line), as well as hooks sold individually without a pre-tied leader.

Naturally, the availability of titanium hooks from Berkeley would be newsworthy in and of itself — at least to anglers. Such a news announcement would be a natural fit for just about any media outlet focused on fishing.

However, given that titanium is also quite strong for its relative weight, you could probably also find specific interest in any media outlet focused on fly fishing. Why? Because using hooks made out of titanium could create new advantages for fly-tying aficionados.

Not only this, but if you had enough lead time, you could probably provide titanium hooks to Journalists at a fly fishing magazine in advance of the actual announcement so they could

- Tie flies using the new titanium hooks, and
- Try out these "titanium flies" to see if they performed any better than "typical" hooks.

And to push a bit further with this concept of looking for multiple "angles" to the same news announcement, it's possible that a Journalist at a business magazine or technology-focused media outlet or a daily newspaper who <u>also happened to be an angler</u> might be convinced that writing about these newfangled titanium hooks would be a good idea.

In other words, if you tweak the story idea, you might get two or more bigger and more impressive story results for the same news announcement.

= =

RULE #29: Pursue Product and/or Service Reviews

Auto Journalists do it. Sewing Journalists do it. Entertainment Journalists do it.

In fact, it seems like nearly every industry has at least a few media outlets that publish Product Reviews — or Service Reviews — as the case may be.

If your objective is ***Publicity Success***, then one of your goals should be figuring out how to land one or more favorable reviews for your company, product and/or service.

Because each industry is different, I'm not going to even begin to try and tell you how to identify which publications, Blogs or TV/Radio/Cable/Web shows are the best ones for you to target. The reality is that by doing a little digging, you can figure out which specific media outlets produce Product and/or Service Reviews.

You should be aware, however, that the larger the media outlet, or the greater the profile or "celebrity" of the reviewer, chances are there will be a process to maneuver through before your product or service can even be considered for a formal review.

Additionally, if you are dealing with Product Reviewers, you need to take into account the monetary value of the product being reviewed. Some media outlets have very strict policies prohibiting them from keeping products after reviews are completed and will want you to handle all aspects of shipping products to/from their location(s). Conversely {*and I have found this to be true with independent reviewers, particularly those that publish reviews on Blogs or on YouTube*}, you may never get your product returned.

This may not be a problem for you if the value of your product is relatively low . . . unless you end up shipping out dozens or hundreds of products to reviewers, then that may be a different matter. On the other end of the spectrum, however, if your product sells for hundreds or thousands of dollars, a Product Review program can cost your firm a large amount of money very quickly.

Regardless, I recommend companies set-aside X-amount of dollars for the expense of products "lost" during the Product Review process each year, however such products may be lost. This way, there will be no budgetary surprises at yearend from your Product/Service Review program(s).

Naturally, the more complicated your product is to use, the greater the likelihood it will have a <u>User Manual</u>.

Hence, if you have a <u>User Manual</u>, I also recommend creating a <u>Product Reviewer Guide</u> — a separate document, both in digital and printed format, designed to walk a Product Reviewer through the review process from A to Z. {***NOTE***: *A Product Reviewer Guide in video format may be an even better approach for you. Just a thought.*}

In closing, here are a couple of final thoughts on how to kick-start a successful Product Review campaign for ***Publicity Success***:

1. **Use a Search Engine** to identify prospective media outlets and reviewers. (While writing this item, I did a search on *Google* for the phrase "fishing line reviews" and got back over 100 million results, ranging from professionally written reviews at *TackleTour.com* and *Sport*

Fishing magazine to amateur-written reviews on Blogs across the Web. I had similar results for a search for "sewing thread reviews," although this search only generated 2.4 million hits. My point is this: If you're not sure where to start, start by searching the Web.)

2. **Don't Ignore Local Newspapers**; they too can be the source of great Product Reviews.

3. **Don't Ignore General Business Media Outlets** either. Media outlets ranging from *The Wall Street Journal* to *Success* magazine and from *CNBC* to *Forbes* regularly publish Product Reviews. Depending upon your product or service lineup, a general business media outlet might be ideal for a Product or Service Review.

4. Last of all, certainly **Don't Forget Reviews Crafted by Your Users**. It's possible that your best Product Reviews will actually be written/produced by your own product users. (Reviews written on *Yelp.com* are a prime example of user-written reviews.) However, you may need to provide users with at least a basic venue for providing such feedback. This can be on a Website, a company *Facebook* Page, or even via a toll-free, call-in line that accepts audio recordings that are then shared on a Webpage as audio recordings or transcribed and shared in written form. Regardless, I recommend you encourage and support end-user feedback that can be deployed as User-generated Reviews.

= = = = = = = = = = = = = = = = = = = =

RULE #30: No Attachments *(Without Prior Permission)*

When emailing a Journalist, Blogger or Analyst, never, never, never send an attachment with your email — EVER!

The one exception to this RULE is **_IF_** you have been given permission in advance to attach a file to your email, then go ahead and send the attachment.

Beyond that? Never! Never! Never!

= = = = = = = = = = = = = = = = = = = =

SECTION 5: FOLLOW-UP

Unfortunately, even if you follow every single RULE in the prior sections absolutely perfectly so that you . . .

- Adopt a *Journalist Mindset,*
- Identify a truly newsworthy "thing," and
- Package it up inside a well-written <u>News Release,</u>
- Create a tightly written, compelling headline, and
- Pitch it to exactly the best Journalist, working for the perfect media outlet, one that is focused on your exact target audience, and you
- Even have great ideas about visual elements for the story . . .

Even then, it's still possible (perhaps even likely), that the Journalist you targeted may not be interested in your story idea. Or she may be interested, but the story may not get published anyway.

In those instances, do NOT give up. Rather, I want you to continue forward.

And that's the purpose of this section, to provide you with the best RULES to teach you how to **FOLLOW-UP**.

= = = = = = = = = = = = = = = = = = = =

RULE #31: Try Again

Chances are the first time you propose a story idea to a Journalist you're going to get turned down. That's okay. It happens even to seasoned Public Relations professionals — a lot. In fact, pretty much everyone gets turned down at least once every day . . . it's a part of life.

That's why your mom probably used this clichéd line of encouragement on you when you experienced disappointment as a child:

If at first you don't succeed, try, try again.

The reason why that statement is a cliché is because of its underlying truism: most people give up way too early and way too easily.

In fact, the vast majority of people who are successful in life are not successful on their very first try. Rather, they are successful specifically because they kept on trying until they became successful. BUT . . . {*and this is very important to understand*}, they typically did not keep doing the same thing over and over. Rather, most successful people try new approaches or methodologies to find out what works.

Case in point: Thomas Edison apparently failed with 10,000 different combinations before discovering the exact configuration required to create a long-lasting filament for the electric light bulb with his 10,001st experiment.

So if you pitched a Journalist on a story angle and you got turned down, here are three things I recommend.

66 RULES for Publicity Success

1. **Evaluate Your Story Angle**: Was it a genuinely newsworthy story idea? If not, come up with a better idea and follow-up with the same Journalist at a future date.
2. **Was It Your Fault?** Perhaps you had a genuinely newsworthy story idea, but your presentation — *your pitch* — was itself flawed. If so, identify the next best Journalist and/or media outlet on your list, tweak your pitch and try again. Remember: Edison didn't keep trying the same thing; he kept tweaking and tweaking until he found the winning formula. {*NOTE: If it was your fault, don't write-off that Journalist. Just make a note and plan to pitch him/her sometime in the future.*}
3. **Was It the Journalist's Fault?** It's possible you simply caught the Journalist at a bad time, during a bad day, or in the middle of a bad week. If so, then make a note of your experience and try pitching that Journalist sometime in the future.

Here's a closing question for this RULE:

How long should you wait before contacting a Journalist again?

That depends. Pitching a story idea to a Journalist is a form of selling, and research shows that we tend to buy from people who we like. Typically, likability comes from trust and rapport, and building trust and rapport tends to take time.

On the one hand, if you are convinced that you have identified the right Journalist, but your pitch fell flat, then you probably need to know what story ideas excite her. That means reading, watching and/or listening to stories she has previously published and then tracking her newest stories as they come out.

As you do so, if you come across a story idea that you believe might be interesting to her, feel free to share it with her — but only if it has nothing to do with you or your company, products or services. The idea here is to GIVE with ZERO expectation of getting anything in return.

Do this a few times and then, when you have a legitimate story idea for her about you or your company, products or services, she'll listen. And as a result, chances are your new pitch will be successful.

= =

RULE #32: Have a Backup Ready to Go *(aka, Try Something Else)*

Sometimes, even if everything has been done correctly, the Fates can conspire against us. In these instances, having a backup plan is a great idea.

Such can be the case with pitching the media.

You might have the perfect story angle, the right Journalist and the best media outlet. But . . . if a similar story was just published by that media property, in all likelihood your pitch is going to get flushed down the tubes.

My recommendation? Always have a backup story idea (or two) in your hip pocket ready to whip out should the need arise.

= =

RULE #33: Make It Easier for Them

Regardless of what you do, sometimes a product, service, invention or topic is just going to be really complicated — perhaps too complicated for a Journalist to wrap his/her head around. If that is the case in your situation, your best bet will be to "write the story" for them.

I don't mean literally write the actual story for the Journalist in question {*although there are times when the best approach is submitting an authored article*}. Rather, I'm suggesting that you do all the advance legwork for them.

By this I mean that you identify all of the answers to the

- Who,
- What,
- When,
- Where,
- Why, and
- How

questions of your story idea.

Ideally, you'll also identify why the readers, listeners and/or viewers of this particular story idea will be interested in reading, listening to and/or watching the finished story.

For good measure, you'll also fold in some outside sources, such as users, customers, partners, etc. Preferably, you'll also offer up some independent third parties, such as industry experts, who can provide an unvarnished viewpoint on your company, products and/or services.

Take all of this, wrap it up with a nice, neat bow, and you've hand-delivered a nearly finished piece for the Journalist in question. In fact, the only thing waiting to be done is actually writing/producing the story.

Well done.

= = = = = = = = = = = = = = = = = = = =

RULE #34: Make It Better for Them

Let's assume that everything has gone well up to this point. In other words, you are very close to achieving ***Publicity Success*** with a nice story published about you, your company and/or products/services for the entire world to see. Cool.

Then as you touch base with the Journalist behind this soon-to-be-published wonder, he mentions, "You know, I really wish I had _____. That would make the story perfect."

And being the savvy business person that you are, you think, "Now what do I do?"

CASE STUDY: *"Milking the Spider"*

Early in my career I had the privilege of working with Natural Product Sciences, an early stage drug discovery firm that was evaluating unique sources for potential pharmaceuticals. One such source: The toxins found in venomous spider bites.

Naturally, getting enough spider venom to be able to work with in a laboratory setting required milking a lot of spiders — an effort akin to milking poisonous snakes versus milking cows. Not surprisingly, NPS was not the only company looking for drug leads from unusual origins; several other firms were examining everything from plants to insects and from mollusks to reptiles for drug leads as well.

In fact, several budding drug firms had turned to nature to bolster their research efforts. And it was this nugget of an idea that we pitched as a possible Trend Story idea to a Business Reporter at the New York Times. *And he loved it!*

101

Five months later, after a fair amount of behind-the-scenes work with this Journalist, he mentioned that the story was now done. But he was missing one thing — artwork — a key visual piece to help him tell the story. Then he asked the critical question:

> *Did I have any ideas that might help him complete the story?*

Unfortunately, I had not even considered writing 66 RULES for Publicity Success *back then, nor had I contemplated RULE #25, so I hadn't really thought "visually" in advance of our pitch to the NYTimes or considered how the right image could help complete this story. Then again, I did know how to think on my feet — so I did.*

"How 'bout a Photo of someone milking a spider?" I asked. "Would that work?"

A few minutes later we had worked out the appropriate details and I took off to set-up a Photo shoot, print the Photo and ship it across country, all within 36 hours. {Yes, this was back before widespread use of email.}

One month later, the story broke on the front page of the Business Section of the New York Times *with the lead Photo showing a close-up image of a lab technician gently holding a spider between padded tweezer tines while the tech also held a tiny glass pipette up to the spider's fangs. Better yet, the Photo caption and credit both noted Natural Product Sciences by name.*

Even better, the NYTimes story broke one day before NPS announced it had closed $5.0 million in a Series A Round of funding.

Having an idea for a Photo, Chart or image isn't the only way you can make a story better for a Journalist, however. In fact, the number of ways you can make the editorial process better are probably limitless — it just requires effort. For example, additional ideas can include

- Recommending industry contacts,
- Suggesting third-party experts/influencers,
- Providing contact information,
- Offering secondary research data, or
- Coordinating interview schedules,

just to name a few.

The important thought is this: You should be prepared to take a good story pitch and transform it into a great story executed very well.

= = = = = = = = = = = = = = = = = = =

BONUS RULE: Say "Thank You"

Few words have the positive influecnce of the phrase "Thank you." Unfortunately, it's an often overlooked phrase, especially in business settings.

So after you complete an interview with a Journalist, don't forget to say "Thank you."

And if/when that interview is morphed into a finished article, Blog post or story, don't forget to say "Thank you" again, this time in the written form.

In today's hyper-connected world, saying "Thank you" to someone via email is accceptable. But if you really want to be remembered by that Journalist, take a few extra minutes to handwrite and mail a "Thank you" card or note.

Believe me — it really will make a difference.

= = = = = = = = = = = = = = = = = = = =

RULE #35: Leverage Your Media Coverage for Increased *Publicity Success*

Congratulations — someone just published the very first article about you, your company or your products/services. That's awesome!

Now what?

Hopefully, you've already taken a few minutes to write and mail a thoughtfully considered "Thank You" note to the Journalist who just helped make you famous. But beyond that, what should you do?

At a minimum, you need to let others know that at least one media outlet considers you, your company and/or your product/service to be a big deal. Probably the easiest way to do this is to include info about the article in the Newsroom on your company Website.

Personally, I recommend creating a subsection within online Newsrooms designed specifically for media coverage, such as something titled "In-the-News" or "Stories" or "Press Coverage." Naturally, if your Website doesn't have a Newsroom already, you'll need to add one, along with the appropriate subsections. {*For more thoughts about Online Newsrooms, see RULE #53 later within these pages.*}

At a minimum, I recommend including the following for every story I found in such "In-the-News" subsections:

1. The **headline** of the story,
2. The **name/logo of the media outlet** that ran the story, and

3. **A hotlink to the original story** on the media outlet's own Website or Blog (as the case may be).

In addition, you may want to snag a line or two from the article to include as a highlight or summary of the published story.

Another example of how to <u>Leverage Your Media Coverage</u> is via eNewsletters.

If you're not using eNewsletters already as a way of staying in touch with your various groups of customers, partners, investors and the like, you should start one right away. They're really quite easy to setup, especially if you use a program like ConstantContact, MailChimp, AWeber or a host of other email applications.

However, once you've got your first eNewsletter ready to go, you definitely should use that platform to let your fans and friends know about your recent media coverage.

Your next step? Go snag your second story!

= = = = = = = = = = = = = = = = = = = =

RULE #36: Repurpose Your Successful Pitches

QUESTION: Have you ever been fishing and caught two or more fish out of the same hole? If so, you already understand the underlying principle behind this RULE.

In other words, if you've already landed a story from one of your story pitches, chances are that same pitch (or a slightly modified version of it) will also land another story from a different Journalist. This likelihood is even greater if that second Journalist

- Works for a different media outlet, and
- Covers a different market than the first Journalist, whether by
  - Geography,
  - Industry, or
  - Both.

When it comes to "repurposing" a successful story pitch, it might just require a tiny tweak. For example, if your company had launched a new mobile app for accepting credit card payments and a Blog focused on managing clothing stores had run a story about your application, then a magazine written for pet store owners could easily run a similar story with very little difficulty.

The truth is that if you own a business that realistically can only sell to prospective customers within a fairly small geography (such as a restaurant with one location), then "repurposing" a successful story pitch will be harder. But that doesn't mean it's impossible — just harder.

In this instance, if you landed a positive restaurant review in your hometown paper, then perhaps there's a regular show on a local TV or radio station that might consider a story about your restaurant. Then again, perhaps there are more than two papers published in your area. If so, have at it.

The point is this: Look for opportunities to repurpose successful media pitches as often, and widely, as possible.

= =

SECTION 6: PUBLICITY 3.0 — EARNED, OWNED AND LEASED OR RENTED MEDIA

Up to this point in <u>66 RULES for Publicity Success</u>, everything has had a direct application toward traditional media relations programs — in other words, getting stories published by Journalists in media outlets they work for, own or control. Industry pros call such Publicity results "Earned Media." To be clear, the remaining RULES in this book focus on Earned Media too.

However, today is a very different world than the one I entered 30-some years ago as a PR professional, especially when it comes to media relations and efforts to produce ***Publicity Success***. In fact, it is hard to envision that Johannes Gutenberg (the acknowledged inventor of the world's first printing press) could have predicted a world where literally everyone on the planet could become — *No*, **IS** — his own Publisher. And that he could be not just a Publisher, but a Citizen-Journalist with the potential of reaching millions of people, even billions, in a matter of minutes.

And this capability is not just limited to people, but has been adopted by millions of organizations worldwide too.

So what do such digital publishing tools and Social Media platforms and services mean to you and your business and its products/services — and to your desires to achieve ***Publicity Success***? Plenty!

First of all, as explained earlier in this book, the World Wide Web and the Social Media applications and platforms that work on the Internet can be incredibly useful Publicity tools. Specifically, such tools/services can be used to identify, target, contact and communicate with Journalists who might be interested in you, your firm and/or your products/services. In fact, using the Web and Social Media to generate media coverage in a traditional media outlet (in print or with a broadcast media property) is really just a twist on what PR pros and savvy business execs have been doing for over 200 years. In other words, it's really **Publicity version 1.0** (as explained in the DEFINITIONS section at the very beginning of this book).

Conversely, **Publicity 2.0** emerged with the birth of Web-based publishing platforms that allowed anyone, regardless of her or his journalistic training, to begin publishing online — first in written form only via popular blogging platforms. Later, this same capability expanded to include online video publishing, especially via *YouTube*, *Vimeo* and others. Such digital-only Journalists and Media Outlets then became media coverage targets for publicists and businesses alike (hence, **Publicity 2.0**).

The continued refinement of such online publishing tools, as well as the explosive adoption of both smartphones and Social Media platforms, has led to what I believe is a new revolution in the publishing world.

Specifically, anyone with texting capabilities on a mobile phone is now a publisher. {*Sounds silly, I know, but it's true!*} Clearly, such publishing capabilities are constrained to other cellphones capable of sending/receiving text messages, but the text messages themselves are, in fact, a form of publishing.

More importantly, the addition of high-speed data capabilities, high-quality displays and high-resolution picture- and video-taking cameras to our mobile phones have transformed them into handheld, portable publishing platforms — devices we now call smartphoncs. But in reality these devices are actually extremely powerful computers.

Add to these smartphones the seemingly ever-expanding publishing and networking capabilities of mobile and online apps, and the birth of **Publicity 3.0** is upon us.

With **Publicity 3.0,** not only can savvy business execs and PR/Marketing types pursue ***Publicity Success*** with Journalists of all types, regardless of where and how they publish to reach their target audiences/publics, but now they can also bypass Journalists and media outlets altogether. And you can follow the exact same path with

1. Media properties that you "own," or via
2. Media properties that you "lease" or "rent."

To be clear, the best examples of Media Properties that an organization can own are its Websites or Blogs. Once you have created a Website or a Blog, it's yours. And whatever you want to publish there is up to you, no one else. In this regard,

You Are the Gatekeeper.

No one else. Not a Reporter. Not an Editor. Not a Producer. Not a Blogger. You!

Conversely, your *Facebook* Page, your company's *Pinterest* account and/or your *YouTube* Channel do not actually belong to you, per sé. In fact, you (or your firm) are merely leasing (or renting) those accounts, with your name on them, from *Snapchat* and *Instagram*, or whatever Social Media service you have "joined."

111

Sure, you get to decide what content, if any, to share with your Friends or Connections on these various Social Media properties via your accounts. And you also get to decide who or what to Follow on these platforms.

But you do NOT get to decide which algorithms, if any, dictate who will see your Photos or videos or messages on "your" Social Media account(s). Or when. Or how often. Or not.

Those decisions are made by the people who run these Social Media services or by the behind-the-scenes software that makes such choices automatically.

You also don't decide what ads or sponsored messages (if any) will run adjacent to (or before) your posts, videos, Photos or content. Such decisions are completely out of your control. In fact, abdicating such control over Social Media advertising, sponsorships and feed-controlling algorithms is, in fact, how you make the rent or lease payments for using someone else's Social Media service.

This being the case, however, does not mean I think that Social Media accounts/services/platforms have no place within the realm of **Publicity 3.0** endeavors. Nothing could be further from the truth.

In fact, many savvy business owners and Publicity professionals utilize Social Media strategies and tactics to generate fantastic ***Publicity Success***, either through traditional and non-traditional Journalists or directly to their target-audience members via such Social Media platforms.

That's why I'm convinced that the technological advancements outlined in the preceding pages are revolutionizing the fields of media relations, public relations, Publicity and journalism. To be clear, you can and should continue to work through traditional and non-traditional Journalists to reach their readers, listeners and viewers, regardless of their publishing platform(s). To me, there is often no faster or less expensive way to reach prospective customers, partners, investors, influencers, employees and others you need to reach than through this means — especially when impartiality is critical to your communications efforts. This is what I mean when I use the terms **Publicity 1.0** or **Publicity 2.0**.

However, when it comes to transforming your business and/or yourself into a publisher, now I'm talking about **Publicity 3.0**, and the implications and potential of **Publicity 3.0** are far-reaching, beyond anything ever possible before.

That's why I've focused this section on **EARNED, OWNED & LEASED/RENTED MEDIA** and the emerging world of **Publicity 3.0**.

= = = = = = = = = = = = = = = = = = = =

RULE #37: You _MUST_ Blog

One of the best ways to attract interest today (including interest from traditional and non-traditional Journalists) is by creating, publishing and distributing new content on a regular basis. And the easiest way to do this is by blogging.

Weblogs (or Blogs for short) had their first beginnings in the mid-1990s, but didn't really begin to take-off until the late 1990s to early 2000s with the launch of such easy-to-use blogging platforms as Blogger, LiveJournal, and WordPress, just to name a few.

The first blogging platforms began as simple, text-heavy, diary- or journal-like services for Web users. Over time these blogging services have evolved to the point that the Websites of many companies are now actually built on these blogging platforms.

One of the more interesting blogging concepts to emerge in the past decade has been the evolution of video blogging, known by some people as vlogging. Some Vloggers (as Video Bloggers are called), have become quite popular and have created very successful businesses around their Vlogs, whether their videos are shot on elaborate sets using expensive video cameras or produced on the cheap using the video-shooting capabilities found in most modern smartphones. One of the advantages of such Vlogs is that someone doesn't need to be a great writer to be successful as a Vlogger (although it helps).

Naturally, some individuals and companies choose to combine both written and visual formats into one Blog, and this is perfectly fine too.

The critical part about blogging — whether word- or video-focused (or both) — is the benefit of being able to use Blogs to become your own Publisher. This capability means <u>you control what and when you publish</u>. You also decide what is worthy of being included on your Blog . . . no one else. Such control is a prime example of some of the benefits of a **Publicity 3.0** world.

Naturally, the more you know about a particular subject, the more your passion will come through in what you publish. Such passion increases the likelihood that you will attract others to your Blog. As a result, this means there is a greater chance that visitors to your Blog will become fans — engaged individuals who care about you, your company, your products/services, your viewpoints, your perspectives, etc. And the more ***engaged*** people are about what you publish, the more likely they are to become fans and/or customers for life.

This fact applies to everyone, including Journalists, because in the end, Journalists are obviously people too.

Yes, the best Journalists have an ethical code to follow that includes maintaining impartiality and the ability to examine everything through a lens of healthy skepticism. But then again, Journalists also have a job to do and that is to produce their own, newsworthy content. And some do so on a multiple-times-a-day basis.

So the easier you make their jobs for them, the more likely Journalists are to produce stories about you, your company, your products, your services and, yes, even your viewpoints. {*And some would argue, especially about your viewpoints.*} This is another benefit of a **Publicity 3.0** approach to your media relations efforts, namely being able to attract and engage directly with traditional and non-traditional Journalists because of what you are publishing on your Blog.

That's where blogging comes into play: it provides you with a platform for publishing and sharing your viewpoints.

To be clear, the point of this RULE is not to try and tell you everything there is to know about blogging. There are bazillions of resources on the Internet this very second available to help you get started with a Blog (if you don't have one or more already in use by you and/or your company).
But I will suggest the following ideas about company Blogs:

1. **Create a schedule and stick to it**. I recommend blogging at least once per week. Less than that and most people will wonder if you're serious about it.

2. **Create an Editorial Calendar**. Depending upon the industry your business operates in, I suspect there are numerous topics that regularly generate interest among customers, partners, investors, industry gurus, Influencers, etc. If so, create your own list of topics to cover in the weeks and months ahead, and then stick to it. {*And if you're not sure where to begin, visit the Websites of a few media outlets that cover your industry and see what topics they're publishing stories about.*}

3. If you're the boss, **_YOU_ Need to Blog**. Please understand — I get that you're busy. So is every other company Founder, President, CEO and General Manager in the world. Get over it. If you want to attract interest from Journalists, the content published on your company Blog has to resonate with your voice. To me, that means that at least once a week, **_YOU_** have to publish something. And if it's too hard or too time-consuming to write a 250- to 750-word piece on a weekly basis (*and I get it, shorter items are typically tougher to write*), then do a Vlog post weekly. Most laptops include a camera built right into them, and if you've got even a basic smartphone, then you've also got a video camera. Just learn how to use it, record your video, then hand it

off to someone on your Marketing team to edit and upload. Or if your Marketing team consists of you, then . . . well, hopefully you get the idea.

4. **Share What You Publish**. At a minimum, let others know about your latest Blog posts via Social Media outreach. Tweet about your posts on *Twitter*, provide updates on *LinkedIn*, upload them to your company's *YouTube* Channel, and share 'em on *Facebook*, *Instagram*, *Pinterest*, etc. And if you're so inclined, share the links to your best posts in your regular company *eNewsletter(s)*.

5. Last of all . . . be sure to give people the opportunity to sign up for **Blog Post Updates** when the latest ones are published.

The decision to begin blogging means that you have entered the **Publicity 3.0** world because you "own" your Blog (or Vlog). In other words, you get to decide what and when you publish (and who you target), with your Blog. That's HUGE because <u>you</u> now have control. And this puts you on a pathway to ***Publicity Success***.

Last of all, make sure the traditional and non-traditional Journalists in your databases know that you're blogging, as this too can help you generate media coverage via your **Publicity 1.0** and **Publicity 2.0** efforts.

= = = = = = = = = = = = = = = = = = = =

RULE #38: Seriously Consider Other "Owned" Media

One of the great underlying values of company Blogs (as described in RULE #37) is that you ***OWN*** the Blog. This means that once you set one up and have a place where it can be hosted, you get to decide everything about it because YOU control it.

You choose the layout, the colors and the publishing schedule. You choose who can edit it and who creates new content for it. You even get to decide if you will allow others to make comments on your Blog. It's <u>ALL</u> up to you.

In a similar vein, these same benefits can be derived from other media platforms you ***OWN***. And it's not like this is something that's a new development, because from my perspective, company brochures, annual reports, flyers, even ads, are each forms of "owned media." The difference is that with Blogs and certain other digital media platforms, once the initial financial investment is made, the media property is yours. And that's way cool (for all the reasons described above.) This is the entire concept behind **Publicity 3.0**.

Given my feelings about Blogs, it should be no surprise then that I feel the same way about any media property that you ***OWN***, but especially digital media.

However, to make sure I am perfectly clear in describing my definition about media properties that you can ***OWN***, I hope you understand that in most instances <u>you **do not** own your account on most Social Media platforms or services</u>.

Sure, you can decide what Photo(s) to upload, what words to use to describe you or your company, or perhaps what background colors or images to select, etc. But make no mistake about it: If *Facebook* decides to change its algorithms or Terms of Service (TOS), you have no say in the matter whatsoever (beyond complaining). And the same concept also holds true for the vast majority of Social Media services/platforms.

In other words, in a very real way, your *Facebook* Page(s) and *LinkedIn* Profile(s)/Page(s) and your *YouTube* Channel(s) and your various accounts on *Twitter, Pinterest, Instagram, Snapchat,* etc., etc., etc. do **NOT** actually belong to you. In reality, they are the property of their respective owners; similarly, your accounts, profiles, pages, etc. are only being lent to you in exchange for the value these Social Media companies derive from you, either now or in the future.

I also want to be very clear on the fact that I am perfectly okay with such arrangements, both for me and for you, as long as we both understand who is in charge here, because it's not us. It's them. But that's absolutely fine because that's a great definition of a free enterprise system:

> *Two or more parties exchange things of value for things of value, and ideally, all parties win.*

But control? Nope. That belongs to the Social Media firms.

So . . . back to this particular RULE and the value of media properties you actually control, and as a result, properties that can be described as media that you **_OWN_**.

Aside from the physical media properties that I described earlier within this RULE, including such things as printed collateral, annual reports and so forth, I believe the list of digital media properties you can **_OWN_** today includes

119

- Websites,
- eNewsletters,
- Podcasts,
- Conference Calls, and
- Webcasts/Webinars.

In each instance, once you pay the fees, you **OWN** each of the digital media properties noted above, whether these are one-time fees or ongoing charges. You may also need to pay usage fees to a third party to host a Website or manage your conference calls or Webcasts, somewhat like paying a toll.

But deciding what is or is not included on a Website? That's your decision. Whether or not to hold a Conference Call, and whom to invite to participate in the call? Well . . . that's your call too {*in more ways than one*}. The same can also be said for eNewsletters, podcasts, Webcasts/Webinars and others.

The bottom line is this,

If you control it *(all of it)*, then you *OWN* it.

And because it's "owned media," you need to understand that with ownership comes great power and potential, especially when it comes to publishing. In other words, if you want to be able to increase your ability to reach and influence Journalists (and thereby increase your chances for **Publicity Success**), I suspect you'll look for additional media properties you can **OWN** and control. That's an example of the power of **Publicity 3.0**.

= = = = = = = = = = = = = = = = = = = =

RULE #39: *LinkedIn* — It's a Social Media "Must Have"

At over 400 million members worldwide, *LinkedIn* has clearly become **the** Social Media leader for professional use (at least within the English-speaking world). In fact, it is now more and more of a rarity to meet someone in business and learn that he or she does not have a *LinkedIn* profile.

However, most businesses and organizations do not have Company Pages on *LinkedIn*. This is a big mistake.

Yes, you can (and should) have a Website for your company. And chances are your company already has a Website (or more than one). That's good.

And yes, most people who are looking for the type of products and/or services your firm offers will likely find it via an Internet search, probably via the *Google* search engine. However, there are times (especially when someone is poking around within *LinkedIn*) that you really need to have a Company Page on *LinkedIn*.

Creating a Company Page on *LinkedIn* is actually quite easy. And if you search within *LinkedIn* for a phrase like "Build a Company Page on *LinkedIn*," you'll find several Posts and slideshows that will walk you through the process step by step.

Once you've launched version 1.0 of your Company Page on *LinkedIn*, you'll want to start creating regular Updates to help

- Attract Followers, and then
- Engage with those Followers

inside the *LinkedIn* universe.

{***NOTE****: I do NOT recommend paying for Sponsored Updates on* LinkedIn *at this early stage for your Company Page. Later? Maybe. Now? No.*}

As you publish your Company Page on *LinkedIn* and then begin producing and publishing Updates to your Company Page, I recommend that you encourage your employees to link to and/or reference your Company Page in their Updates and Posts. And don't forget to let them know it's okay for them to share Updates from the Company Page too. Naturally, these are steps you and your Marketing team members should be taking as well.

Additionally, be sure to utilize *LinkedIn* Analytics to monitor your progress as you recruit and engage with Followers, while also looking for ways to improve your *LinkedIn* success.

As you may have recognized, however, everything I've written within this RULE up to this point applies to any business owner from a **Publicity 3.0** standpoint, an approach that allows you to reach prospective and current customers, partners, investors, employees and more through content/messages that you control.

This being the case, it's also critical for me to address ways that you can apply these same principles to the world of media relations and Publicity, especially when it comes to generating ***Publicity Success*** with both traditional and non-traditional Journalists.

So . . . because *LinkedIn* has become the *de facto* Social Media platform for business professionals around the world, it should not be too surprising to learn that the number of Journalists with *LinkedIn* profiles is actually quite large.

Case in point, three *LinkedIn* searches I performed moments ago returned results showcasing

- Nearly 1.6 million Editors,
- 1+ million Producers, and
- 400,000+ Reporters.

The challenge then becomes finding the right Journalists (who are also members of LinkedIn) for you and your firm. Thankfully, the tools within *LinkedIn* make this process relatively easy. Here's how to get started:

First, log into *LinkedIn*. Then enter the term you want to look for within the search window near the top of the page, for example, the title "Reporter." {***NOTE***: *When I do this, I end up with over 400,000 results across my entire* LinkedIn *network, clearly way too many Reporters for me to reasonably track/approach. Naturally, your results may vary.*}

The way to manage such a massive list of Reporters is to begin a filtering process to make the list more user-friendly. To do this, look to the left side of the page. Here you'll note an Advanced Search column featuring a wide variety of filtering categories that you can use to help narrow your search. These categories range from Location to Company Name and from Industry to a number of Premium Filters. Such Premium Filters can only be used if you pay for such additional capabilities by becoming a Premium subscriber to *LinkedIn*. {***NOTE***: *I am a Premium subscriber; you may want to become one too.*}

However, by doing something simple like adding "United States" as a Country filter within *LinkedIn*, the number of Reporters in my search results was lowered to fewer than 200,000.

When I added "Newspapers" as another filter, however, the number dropped to less than 20,000 Reporters.

But . . . {*and here's an example of where it starts to get fun*} . . . when I added an additional filter to my search, in this case *Dow Jones* as the Current Company, the number of Reporters working at *Dow Jones* within my *LinkedIn* network dropped to a total of 18.

Now that's a number I can manage!

Further, when I clicked on the top *Dow Jones* Reporter within my *LinkedIn* search results — Jared Diamond — I saw all sorts of things about Jared, such as

- His beat (Sports, but especially the New York Mets),
- Ways to contact him (including a phone number and his personal *Twitter* handle),
- His previous employers,
- And more.

That's cool!

Another way to narrow down your search results within *LinkedIn* is to manually enter your own Keyword search term.

To do this, go back to your initial search results page when you filtered using the title Reporter. {*You'll remember that my results for this search generated over 400,000 Reporters within my* LinkedIn *network.*}

Near the very top of the Advanced Search column on the left side of the page you should see the title "Reporter" inside the field named Keywords, correct? Good.

Immediately to the right of the title "Reporter," type this term:

+ Computer

Then hit the Return (or "Enter") key on your keyboard.

When I do this, my search results immediately dropped to just over 1,000 Reporters, down from 400,000+ Reporters. And that's without any additional filtering.

When I add in "United States" and *"Dow Jones"* as additional filters, I end up with just one (1) result — *Jim Carlton, a San Francisco-based Reporter at* The Wall Street Journal — who (among other topics) covers the Computer industry.

Once you start to play around with manual filtering within *LinkedIn's* search functions, you can come up with all sorts of interesting results.

> {*Case in point: My wife is into all aspects of sewing. So when I perform a* LinkedIn *search across my network looking for Reporters in the "United States" that work in the "Apparel & Fashion" Industry with the additional keyword of "Sewing," I end up with 38 Reporters+Sewing. Neat, huh?*}

Please note that as you begin down this path of identifying Journalists within *LinkedIn* who may be interested in your company, not everyone you find may be a Journalist <u>today</u> or a person who covers your particular industry <u>today</u>. Even so, if they covered your industry in the past, they may do so at some point in the future.

More importantly, they will at least be somewhat aware of (or a fan of) your industry. So do not consider such search results worthless, as they may in fact prove quite valuable — *either now or in the future.*

My point is this:

**If you want to achieve *Publicity Success*,
you HAVE TO be on *LinkedIn*. Period.**

And now . . . *perhaps* . . . you have learned some new tips on
how to make *LinkedIn* more valuable for you in your Publicity
efforts.

= = = = = = = = = = = = = = = = = = = =

RULE #40: *YouTube* — It's a Social Media "Must Have"

It's estimated that over 4,000,000,000 *YouTube* videos are watched each and every day. That's four BILLION — with a "**B**."

Given that the emergence of online video has only taken place in the last 10-12 years, that is just crazy, silly growth! And given Alphabet's expectations, those *YouTube* views will continue to grow exponentially for the foreseeable future.

Obviously, with over one billion users worldwide, *YouTube* has become an amazing phenomenon in a little more than a decade. As such, online video in general, and *YouTube* videos specifically, have become *de rigueur* in Marketing departments and agencies all over the planet. I concur; companies should be using *YouTube* for all sorts of Marketing and sales purposes.

But given that <u>66 RULES for Publicity Success</u> is about being successful in your Publicity and PR campaigns, it might be surprising to you to learn that I believe that *YouTube* is already a component of your PR/Publicity Programs — even if you DO NOT have your own *YouTube* Channel today.

"What?" you ask. "How is that possible?"

Let me explain.

The reality is that any Journalist worth his/her salt is going to research you, your company, its people and your products/services, partners, investors, etc. before officially starting to write and/or produce his/her story. And the bigger the potential story, the deeper and wider they will dig to learn all they can before they begin writing/reporting.

And that means she/he will turn to search engines to find out whatever they can learn about the "collective" you.

> **QUICK***: Any guess as to the second largest Search Engine on the planet? Yup — it's* YouTube.
>
> *As of February 2016, over 3 billion searches are performed on* YouTube *each month. Crazy, huh?*

So . . . if a Journalist is going to research your company before writing a story, what do you think the chances are he/she will take a few seconds to see what results they can find on *YouTube* about you and your company? Yeah, probably pretty good.

Now, will it destroy you (or the story), if your company doesn't have its own *YouTube* Channel? Probably not. But it would definitely be a lost opportunity from a Publicity/PR standpoint. {*And that doesn't even take into consideration lost Marketing and sales opportunities for you and your firm.*}

Truth is, the larger your firm, the greater the likelihood there will be one or more videos that have been uploaded onto *YouTube* about you, your company and/or your products/services <u>even if YOU DON'T have your own *YouTube* Channel</u>.

{**NOTE***: Don't believe me? Check it out. Go right now and search to see if there are any videos about you, your company and/or your products/services already uploaded onto* YouTube. *The larger your company, the greater the likelihood this is true.*

{<u>*Case in point*</u>*: I just performed a* YouTube *search for a grocery store based in Texas and Mexico called HEB, and I conducted my search using the search phrase "HEB grocery store." As it turns out, HEB has its own* YouTube *Channel (something I didn't know) with over 225 videos already uploaded onto it. But (and this fact helps make my point), it turns* *out that 18 of the first 20 videos that show up for an "HEB grocery store" search within* YouTube *are NOT from HEB. Interesting, huh?*}

If you already have a *YouTube* Channel, then ask yourself if you've been using your Channel for Publicity and/or PR purposes? If not, then start doing so — now.

How? At a minimum, I'd recommend creating and uploading onto your *YouTube* Channel three types of short (sub-three minute) videos. These are

- <u>Executive Biography Videos</u>,
- <u>Get to Know Us Videos</u>, and
- <u>Product/Service Introductory Videos</u>.

<u>Executive Biography Videos</u>: I'd shoot these as if each executive was being interviewed by a Journalist. Ideally, I'd have another person off-camera asking questions, with the executive being interviewed facing the interviewer and not the camera.

Questions for these <u>Executive Biography Videos</u> should center on providing info into the executive's background, his/her responsibilities and his/her vision for helping move the company forward. I'd probably also throw in a personal question or two to hopefully create *relate-ability* to each executive, perhaps something like *"What's something you like to do for fun?"* or *"What's the craziest thing you've ever done?"*

<u>Get to Know Us Videos</u>: For these videos, I recommend having the top executive from your firm on-camera providing a quick overview of the company, its market and its products/services. For these <u>Get to Know Us Videos</u>, I believe it is best for the executive to look directly into the camera (when she/he is actually on-camera). Additionally, it is quite

okay to also use portions of the audio recording to provide a voiceover, narrator-like feel to parts of these videos.

Product/Service Introductory Videos: These videos are designed to provide short, snapshot overviews for specific products, services and/or Product/Service Lines. They do not require having an executive or employee on-camera, but I do recommend having an audio track (at a minimum).

Naturally, once you've got these videos produced, upload them to your *YouTube* Channel as soon as possible. And (presuming you already have a media outreach program in place), shoot out a quick email to your editorial database(s) to provide Journalists with a heads-up that these videos are now available on your company's *YouTube* Channel.

Beyond this, consider producing videos for some of your news announcements and uploading these to your *YouTube* Channel too. At a minimum, I believe that links to such videos should be included inside any document/file you produce and distribute to members of the media, such as News Releases, Media Alerts, Facts Sheets, etc.

If, however, you're **a *YouTube* Channel newcomer** (like I was) and you don't have a *YouTube* Channel for your company (or yourself), get one. It takes only a few minutes to get the most basic Channel set up on *YouTube*.

Specifically, go online to *Google.com* and type the following phrase into the *Google* search window:

"creating a YouTube channel."

When you do, the first result will walk you through the short process for creating a *YouTube* Channel and will also provide you with a hotlink to a *Google* URL that delivers additional details. Beyond that, you'll see that there are over 100 million additional online results when you search for the phrase "creating a *YouTube* channel." So feel free to peruse further, should you choose to do so.

Then (at a minimum) produce and upload onto your new *YouTube* Channel <u>Executive Biography Videos</u>, <u>Get to Know Us Videos</u> and <u>Product/Service Introductory Videos</u> as noted earlier within this RULE.

You'll then be on your way to using *YouTube* as a vehicle for ***Publicity Success*** — from **Publicity 3.0** all the way back to **Publicity 1.0**.

*{**NOTE**: If you're not an expert in video production, don't sweat it. There are millions and millions of How To videos uploaded onto* YouTube *that will walk you through every step of the process — even if you're only a beginner.}*

= = = = = = = = = = = = = = = = = = = =

RULE #41: *Twitter* — It's a Social Media "Must Have"

If you've already got a *LinkedIn* Page and a *YouTube* Channel for your business, chances are you've got a *Twitter* account (or two or three) for your company too.

And when it comes to pursuing ***Publicity Success***, you must be on *Twitter*, both personally and professionally. In other words, you must have at least one *Twitter* account for your company.

Within the **Publicity 3.0** world, please remember that you do NOT get to make the final decisions on every aspect of your *Twitter* accounts — *Twitter* does. You are merely renting/leasing those accounts from *Twitter*, and you make such payments by allowing the company to interrupt your *Twitter* feed with sponsored content.

Additionally, given *Twitter*'s Terms of Service (TOS), you've also given *Twitter* the right to decide if any or all of the tweets you share via your account are illegal or offensive. If they are deemed so, *Twitter* can and will delete the illegal or offensive materials and/or accounts, as it has done thousands of times with *Twitter* accounts it believed were spreading terrorist messages and/or propaganda.

Nevertheless, the value of *Twitter* is the ability to directly reach and communicate with targeted audience members, bypassing both traditional and non-traditional Journalists and the media outlets they work for. This capability is huge.

Additionally, I also recommend identifying and following key Journalists that report on your industry. As noted back in RULE #9, searching within *Twitter* via https://search.twitter.com, is a great way to look for and find the right Journalists for your company.

Additionally, I think it's smart to identify and research lists of *Twitter* Journalists that cover your industry. *(See page 38.)*

= = = = = = = = = = = = = = = = = = =

BONUS RULE: *Instagram — Another Social Media MUST HAVE!*

As of the beginning of 2016, Instagram *had more than 400 million users, which means it's now larger than* Twitter *and nearly as large as* LinkedIn. *And despite what some people may tell you,* Instagram *is no longer JUST for personal use. In fact, more and more businesses are adopting* Instagram *everyday . . . and with great success.*

As noted in the previous pages, you will achieve **Publicity Success** *for your business by helping drive people and organizations to action, and in the process, you will increase the value of your organization, products/services and/or yourself.*

And if that's your desired outcome, then Instagram *can definitely DRIVE ACTION; that's why* IG *is another* **must have** *in my book as it's clearly a platform for* **Publicity 3.0** *programs and success.*

To be clear, as a Social Media platform, Instagram *falls into the category of media properties that individuals and organizations do NOT own. Rather, such accounts are merely* <u>rented</u> *or* <u>leased</u>, *which means that* Instagram *(or more correctly, its parent company,* Facebook*) decides what rules govern these Social Media properties.*

Such was the case in early 2016 when Instagram *moved away from feeding chronological images and videos directly to you from people and businesses you had decided to follow and instead began delivering images/video to users based upon decisions made by algorithms. In other words, special math programs now decide what images appear in the image feeds of all* Instagram *account holders. And that's* IG's *right, given its Terms of Service (TOS) That decision by* Instagram/Facebook, *something completely out of your control, is a precise example of what I mean when I say you only lease or rent your* Instagram *accounts.*

Nevertheless, Instagram *allows organizations and people to reach millions and millions of prospective or existing customers, partners, investors, employees and more, bypassing both traditional and non-traditional Journalists and media outlets — and that's HUGE!*

So . . . if your business isn't "on" Instagram *yet, then you need to get that fixed . . . TODAY!*

Additionally, if you're not on IG as a business professional — even IF you already have a personal Instagram *account — I would sign up for a "professional" IG account as the Founder, CEO, President or whatever-your-title-is-executive for your business . . . TODAY! Why? Because IG allows any business leader to simply and easily reach existing and prospective employees, investors, partners and customers more directly, with your "voice" and your messages, bypassing traditional and non-traditional Journalists and media outlets alike in the process.*

My Bottom Line: *If you're not on Instagram, personally, get there — now. And if your company/organization is not on* IG *either, then make it happen . . . now.*

To be clear, I will not use this BONUS RULE to tell you all the ins and outs of Instagram *and how to use it for your benefit, bussiness-wise.*

However, I just did perform an online search on "How to use Instagram *for your business" and* Google *produced over 60 million results for me. So if you want to learn how to use* Instagram *for your business, go to* Google *first.*

However, the second place you should go is to IG *itself; in other words, use* Instagram *as its own search engine. Begin poking around; look for people and topics of interest to you and your business. Chances are you'll be really surprised at how much you can find and learn on* Instagram *itself.*

Then take what you've already learned about producing **Publicity Success** *and apply those lessons to Instagram.*

Last thing: In case you did not know this, Instagram *does allow you to use hashtags.* {You know, those Internet thingies with a "pound sign" in front of a word, like this: #instagram.} *In fact,* Instagram *allows users to include up to 30 hashtags per Post.*

Hence, if you have ANY interest whatsoever in generating **Publicity Success** *on* Instagram, *you have to use hashtags as that will be the most likely way that people will find your* IG *account — and your scintillating and engaging content.*

{**NOTE:** Would I use 30 hashtags every time? Probably not. Then again, I have used 30 hashtags numerous times.

Now that *IG* is using algorithms to define what content is seen by whom and when, I suspect we'll learn in the not too distant future if there is an ideal range of hashtags to use with *IG* posts.

Regardless, the maximum number of hashtags you can use per post on Instagram today is 30.}

= =

RULE #42: Every Other Social Media Service/Platform is a Maybe — *(Deciding When a Social Media "Maybe" is Actually a Social Media "Must Have")*

Beyond the most widely used ones — *Facebook, YouTube, LinkedIn, Twitter, Instagram, Snapchat, Pinterest* — there are actually thousands of Social Media services and platforms in operation today . . . and that's just in the English-speaking world.

Each of these platforms is vying for your attention each and every moment of every single day, whether for personal or professional use. And many of these other Social Media platforms are quite valuable — *personally* — and can be valuable (from a Marketing standpoint) for professional reasons as well, including selling stuff and Marketing your products/services.

BUT . . . because this is a book about generating ***Publicity Success***, my question then for you is this,

> *Can a particular Social Media service or platform help you be successful in generating media coverage?*

And at the risk of being accused of waffling, the answer is

It Depends.

The reason my answer is "it depends" is because each business and its owners and its age and its circumstances and its mixture of products/services and its customers and its location . . . and, and, and . . . are different from every other business out in the great, big world.

Case in point: With her undergraduate degree in Clothing and Textiles from Brigham Young University, my wife has become a pretty accomplished quilter. In fact, she worked for several years for a successful retailer in Sandy, Utah called Quilt Etc.

As most readers might suspect, the vast majority of quilters are women. In fact the latest study from QUILTS, INC. (producers of the largest quilt industry trade shows in the world) says that 100% of all quilters who spend at least $600 per year on quilting are women. Similarly, the latest data shows that over 85% of all *Pinterest* users are also women.

Given the combination of such information, I'm confident that *Pinterest* would make an excellent choice of a Social Media platform for Quilt Etc. In this regard, Quilt Etc. could easily use *Pinterest* to promote

- Quilting patterns it is selling,
- Classes it is giving,
- Favorite products its employees and instructors use, and
- More.

Quilt Etc. could also encourage engagement with quilters all over the world via *Pinterest,* including with Journalists who are quilters or who cover the quilting industry.

And it's that last portion of that previous sentence — *(engaging) with Journalists who are quilters or who cover the quilting industry —* that I find most interesting when it comes to producing **Publicity Success**. In other words, from a **Publicity 3.0** standpoint, *Pinterest* is an ideal vehicle for directly communicating with female customers, prospective customers, employees, partners, investors and more — and this communications aspect is valuable for a business like Quilt Etc. But *Pinterest* can also attract interest from traditional and non-traditional Journalists and lead to media coverage in traditional and online-only media, as well as across Social Media platforms.

However, would *Pinterest* be a smart choice for a small, custom software development shop trying to drum up media coverage? Chances are that unless that software development shop was owned/run by (or targeted at) women, probably not. Why? For two reasons, at least.

One reason is because the focus of *Pinterest* is on sharing images with others (both stills and videos). And although the amount of Infographics shared on *Pinterest* has skyrocketed in the past few years (especially in business-related categories), the reality is that custom software development does not naturally lend itself to beautiful imagery. It can, but in reality, it's not highly likely.

Two, I suspect that the vast majority of decision-makers who can and do hire custom software development shops continue to be men. Given that the primary users of *Pinterest* are women, *Pinterest* would be a mismatch, gender-wise, when it came to trying to attract prospective media coverage of custom software development.

Nevertheless, is it possible to find a female Journalist on *Pinterest* who covers custom software development who eventually covers your company after following your custom software development firm on *Pinterest?* Maybe.

However, is it possible to begin with zero connection with a particular Journalist and, through your activities within a Social Media platform, begin a process that leads to generating media coverage by/through that Journalist? To me, the answer is a resounding YES!

Am I suggesting that such outcomes will occur only because you began using *Pinterest, Instagram, Snapchat,* etc.? Of course not, especially since any Journalist worth his/her salt will always conduct additional research on any subject BEFORE beginning to write/produce a story.

Nevertheless, can *Pinterest, Instagram, Snapchat* and other Social Media services serve as the impetus for the beginning of a Publicity adventure? Absolutely!

Now the question for you to consider is which, if any, of the myriad of other Social Media platforms will serve your business best for ***Publicity Success*** — not counting your Blog, *Facebook, LinkedIn, YouTube, Twitter* or *Instagram* accounts?

Unfortunately, my answer still remains . . .

It Depends.

So I'll leave that decision up to you.

= = = = = = = = = = = = = = = = = = = =

RULE #43: Sponsored Content *(Should You Do It)?*

To be clear, RULE #43 is NOT about the question of whether or not your company should pay for Sponsored Content on Websites or Social Media platforms for Marketing or sales purposes. To me, that's a question for your Marketing and sales teams. Besides, such a question is not the focus of 66 RULES for Publicity Success.

However, from a Publicity-generating perspective, this is an interesting question:

> *Should you pay for Sponsored Content to attempt to generate favorable media coverage?*

For the record, my first thought when I considered this RULE and this question was a very clear "absolutely not!" and that's probably due in large part to my Mass Communications studies at BYU over 30 years ago. Back then there was clearly a well-defined line of demarcation between Public Relations and Advertising, as well as between each of the various Marketing disciplines.

But that was then and this is now, and such lines of demarcation . . . well . . . to say they have blurred would be an oversimplification.

Case in point, what is one of the major news story lines each and every January (or occasionally in February)? Okay, yes, it's coverage of the Super Bowl.

But you can also guarantee that each year there will be tons and tons of stories, Blog posts, tweets, shares and more about the best commercials run during the Super Bowl. In other words, stories about ads.

And to be blunt, what is Sponsored Content if not another form of an advertisement? And have I seen media coverage of Sponsored Content? All the time.

The most common form of Sponsored Content generating Publicity for the sponsoring company is in the form of Bloggers writing about, and Social Media mavens sharing, said Sponsored Content on their Blogs/Websites and/or via their Social Media accounts.

So . . . have I changed my tune? Should companies use Sponsored Content to try and achieve ***Publicity Success***?

Today I believe the answer to this question is (as it was in RULE #42) . . .

It Depends.

And the reason my answer is "it depends" is the same as it was back in RULE #42. In other words, each business and its owners and its age and its circumstances and its mixture of products/services and its customers and its location and, and, and, are different from every other business out in the great, big world.

Additionally, I also believe that your choice to utilize Sponsored Content to try and generate ***Publicity Success*** also depends upon whether or not you have (or can create) compelling content that will attract attention from Journalists, Bloggers and Social Media mavens. If you do (or can), fantastic! In other words, I can also make an argument that Sponsored Content falls within the boundaries of **Publicity 3.0** strategies.

{*Yes, I recognize that some Marketing and Advertising purists will take exception to my suggestion here.*}

Nevertheless, in my opinion, I believe it's clear that Sponsored Content can be another pathway to ***Publicity Success*** for many firms — it just depends on if your business can benefit from such an approach.

However, without compelling content in hand, Sponsored Content makes no sense for any business (in my opinion). In other words, if you do not have (or cannot create compelling content), chances are Sponsored Content will be a waste of your money and time from a Marketing and sales standpoint too. And why would you want to do that anyway?

So . . . should you use Sponsored Content in an effort to generate ***Publicity Success***?

I believe this is something every organization should seriously consider. But for your business? It depends.

= = = = = = = = = = = = = = = = = = = =

RULE #44: Online Advertising — *(Should You Do It)*?

When it comes to Marketing and sales in today's world, using online advertising is a no-brainer — especially when you take into account the ability to micro-segment the individuals targeted with your advertising messages to very tightly defined demographic market segments.

So if you want to target online ads at women between the ages of 25 and 30 who live in the borough of Brooklyn in New York City, watch *The Bachelor*, and are graduates of NYU . . . that's doable.

The question, however (as explained in RULE #43), is this:

Can you achieve **Publicity Success**
<u>through</u> online advertising programs?

If the answer to this question is affirmative, then the follow-on question is fairly straightforward:

Should you do it?

Given my take in RULE #43, you might be surprised by my feelings regarding these questions.

Specifically, I believe because it is possible to narrow-down your targeted online advertising recipients so tightly, so precisely, that yes, companies should definitely consider using online advertising as a tool for achieving ***Publicity Success***. {*Again, I believe this is another aspect of viewing the world through a* ***Publicity 3.0*** *lens.*}

Then again, I also believe another approach to online advertising with a goal of achieving ***Publicity Success*** could be identifying and delivering nuanced advertising to very, very small segments of Journalists with information about your company, products/services, etc. with the goal of eventually having such Journalists write about you, your company, etc.

In other words, think of micro-segmented online advertising as one early step in what may end up being a long, long process.

When approached from this perspective, then I believe the answer should be yes — *do it* — use online advertising to micro-target Journalists with appropriate messages about your company and its products/services. {*Interesting thought, huh?!?!*}

= = = = = = = = = = = = = = = = = = = =

SECTION 7: THINK BEFORE YOU . . .

As I was contemplating what concepts to cover in this section of 66 RULES for Publicity Success, it occurred to me that today's hyper-connected, *speed wins*, go-go-go world is fraught with danger for everyone, from business owners to Marketing professionals, as well as from students to average employees. And the reason why is simple:

> *The technology revolution means that anything that happens anywhere can reach virtually everyone on the planet in a matter of minutes.*

This is our new reality, a reality driven by over 7.2 billion mobile phones, the vast majority of which can take pictures, shoot videos and are connected to the Internet. And when it comes to trying to achieve **Publicity Success**, you have to understand both

- This fact (as described above), and
- The implications of this fact.

Namely, what you do (or don't do) matters — A LOT. So much so that on the positive side, your actions (or inactions) can transform your business into a household name overnight. And on the negative side, your actions (or inactions) can force you to close your business — or worse.

Please understand: I am NOT trying to freak you out. I am merely stating the facts so you understand what is at stake here. And that's why it's crucial that you **think before you** . . . .

= = = = = = = = = = = = = = = = = = = =

RULE #45: Think Before You Text

As of early 2016, industry estimates suggest there are over 7.2 billion cell phones on the planet (as noted at the beginning of this section). In other words, that's more phones than people.

According to the latest figures available from Forrester Research, cell phone users in the United States send more than 2 trillion text messages each year. And SMS usage in other regions of the world are much higher than here in the U.S. In fact, we're pikers by comparison.

Just as it's quite easy to send a text message out to a group, it's also quite easy to forward a text message to another person or to a new group (even if it's just a "cut and paste" job).

And that's the concern: Once the *SEND Button* has been pushed there is no *UNDO Button* to bring back (or destroy) that

- One inappropriate statement,
- One cutting comment,
- One secret disclosed,
- One hurtful thought,
- Etc.

The cautionary tale? Once you've written that text or SMS message and pushed the *SEND Button*, you can NEVER, EVER bring back that message.

In other words:

Think before you text.

= =

147

RULE #46: Think Before You Blog

Do you know the term *"Dooced"?*

It means to get **fired for what you've written on a Blog** (or Website).

The term comes from the now famous blog *Dooce.com* written by Heather Armstrong, who was fired for things she wrote about her then place of employment (back in 2002).

The good news for Armstrong was that after getting fired for what she'd written, she was able to transform her negative experience into a full-time gig that supported her family.

The bad news is that not everyone else in similar straits has been quite so fortunate.

> {*NOTE: As of this writing,* **over 75 million results** *come up when you search for the two words "fired" and "blog" on* Google.}

The cautionary tale? Be careful what you blog about.

In other words:

Think before you blog.

= = = = = = = = = = = = = = = = = = = =

RULE #47: Think Before You Tweet

In October 2009, NFL Pro Bowl running back Larry Johnson was released by the Kansas City Chiefs, just 75 yards short of breaking the team career rushing record of Priest Holmes.

What was the proverbial straw that broke the camel's back and the patience of team ownership and management? According to the *Associated Press*, it was Johnson's tweet where he insulted fans, attacked his coach and used a gay slur.

A recent *Google* search for the words "fired" and *Twitter* generated over 115 million hits.

Scan through the first few pages of these search results and you'll find numerous articles about individuals fired because of something they tweeted about on *Twitter*.

The cautionary tale? Be careful what you write on *Twitter*.

In other words:

Think before you tweet.

= = = = = = = = = = = = = = = = = = = =

RULE #48: Think Before You Share that Photo

Perhaps you're thinking, "Well, this RULE doesn't apply to me because I use *Snapchat* or some other application that deletes Photos after they're opened." In which case you'd be right, but then again, you'd also be absolutely wrong at the exact same time.

Why? Just because an image is "deleted" from your phone does NOT mean that it has been deleted forever off the servers used by the cellular provider.

Nor does it prevent someone from screengrabbing a *Snapchat* image or video, saving it and/or sharing it with others. More importantly, even "deleted" files can often be restored by someone with enough time and the proper training and resources.

For example, any idea how easy it is to "permanently" capture an image on your smartphone, even if that image is slated to disappear momentarily off your phone? If you don't know about this, look up the term "screenshot" on *Wikipedia*.

The reality is that if you've shared a Photo somewhere on the Web (via a Social Media platform or via email), such images are even harder to permanently delete.

The better counsel is this: Be careful about the Photos you upload onto the 'Net. In other words:

Think before you upload that Photo.

= =

RULE #49: Think Before You Upload that Video

Not too long ago, I spoke at a local university as a guest lecturer for an introductory Mass Communications class.

One of my recommendations for the students was this:

> *Go check out your* Facebook, Twitter, Instagram, *and* Pinterest *accounts, as well as any other Social Media accounts you might be using, and* <u>*delete any videos you would be too embarrassed to have your grandmother watch*</u>.

Unfortunately, the advances in technology have made it extremely easy to shoot video almost anywhere and then upload them to the Web for all to see — including

- Employers,
- Headhunters,
- Prospective employers,
- College Admissions officers,
- Friends,
- Family members,
- Spouses (and prospective spouses),
- And more.

The cautionary tale? Be careful what videos you upload onto the Web.

In other words:

Think before you upload a video.

= = = = = = = = = = = = = = = = = = = =

RULE #50: Think Before You Update ANY Social Media Site

What does it tell you when a *Google* search for the phrase "Social Media Firing" returns more than 20 million results?

Hopefully, it tells you to be careful about what you share on Social Media platforms.

One infamous example of someone who broke this RULE comes from the United Kingdom where a young woman posted the following complaint on *Facebook* about her boss:

> *OMG I HATE MY JOB!! My boss is a total pervvy wanker always making me do $%@* stuff just to piss me off!! WANKER!*

Unfortunately for the young lady in question, her boss was apparently one of her Friends on *Facebook*. Uh oh!

And then he replied to her Wall Post, firing her on the spot — via *Facebook*. {*Turns out she still had two weeks left in her six-month probationary trial period at work!*} DOUBLE UH OH!

The cautionary tale? Anything you publish on a social networking platform can — *and likely will* — be shared on Social Media and beyond, whether you want it to be shared or not. Clearly, be very careful when you update *Facebook*, *LinkedIn*, *Twitter* or any other social networking platform.

In other words:

Think before you update ANY Social Media site.

= = = = = = = = = = = = = = = = = = = =

RULE #51: Think Before You Do *ANYTHING* in Public

The memorial service for Nelson Mandela was being held in FNB Stadium in Johannesburg, South Africa. Given Mandela's worldwide societal impact, it was truly a somber affair. {*Well, at least it was for most people at the event.*}

However, Photographers in attendance caught U.S. President Barack Obama posing for a "Selfie" snapshot with Denmark's Prime Minister Helle Thorning-Schmidt and British Prime Minister David Cameron . . . **during the funeral services!**

Unfortunately, many Photographers (and Videographers) also captured images of Obama's wife, Michelle, off to the side, looking stern and very unhappy. Ouch! {*You can see examples of this arguably non-Presidential moment by searching either on* YouTube *or within virtually any search engine.*}

Here's the lesson every executive and entrepreneur needs to understand about this RULE:

> *The greater your visibility, notoriety or success, whether*
> *as an individual or as an organization, the more*
> *careful you must be when you go out in public.*

Should President Obama have known better than to pose for a three-way Selfie DURING Mandela's memorial service? Of course! The same can also be said for PM's Cameron and Schmidt.

Clearly, the higher up the celebrity or public official food chain one gets, the greater the likelihood that everything you do will be chronicled by those around you: by professional Journalists, by Paparazzi and by others simply looking to make a name for themselves.

In other words:

Think before you do ANYTHING in public.

= = = = = = = = = = = = = = = = = = = =

SECTION 8: OTHER TOOLS & ACTIVITIES

If your goal is to produce positive Publicity results, then there are definitely other products and services you should consider as possible tools in your tool chest, a few of which are included in this section.

In addition, I've also outlined a handful of Publicity activities you might consider as part of an overall Public Relations Plan.

= =

RULE #52: Commercial Wire Services — You Should Use One

If you're writing (and distributing) News Releases, Media Alerts, public statements and/or News Briefs, I seriously recommend you *use a Commercial Wire Service*.

The best Commercial Wire Services have relationships with all of the leading media outlets and the top search engines on the Internet. As a result, by using a Commercial Wire Service, you **virtually guarantee** at least a minimum level of online "pick-up" and/or coverage of your announcement.

> {*NOTE: IF YOU WORK FOR (OR REPRESENT) A PUBLICLY TRADED COMPANY, YOU CAN NOW "GET AWAY WITH"* **NOT** *USING A COMMERCIAL WIRE SERVICE TO MEET THE* **TIMELY** *AND* **FULL-DISCLOSURE** *REQUIREMENTS OF THE* **UNITED STATES SECURITIES AND EXCHANGE COMMISSION (SEC)** *WHEN YOU DISTRIBUTE "NON-PUBLIC" NEWS THAT IS ALSO CONSIDERED "MATERIAL" IN NATURE . . .* **IF** *. . .*

> • *YOU GIVE PRIOR NOTICE TO THE WORLD THAT YOU INTEND TO USE WEB-BASED SERVICES, INCLUDING COMPANY WEBSITES OR OTHER FORMS OF DIGITAL MEDIA (E.G., SOCIAL MEDIA SERVICES) FOR DISTRIBUTING MATERIAL NEWS AND INFORMATION.*}

Now for the record, I do **NOT** recommend ***just*** using a Commercial Wire Service for News Release distribution.

Historically, I have actually used four different methods for distributing news and information, and wire services are just

one of the four I have utilized (the three other vehicles being email, mail/delivery service and hand-delivery.)
Commercial Wire Service companies I've used include

1. PR Newswire,
2. Business Wire,
3. PR Web, and
4. Marketwire.

I tend to like PR Newswire and Business Wire the most as I believe they have the largest and most comprehensive media outlets connections in the Commercial Wire Service marketplace. But feel free to use any service you wish.

= =

RULE #53: Build & Maintain an Online Newsroom

I have no misgivings, whatsoever, about this RULE:

Every company needs an Online Newsroom.

No question about it.

If you're reading this book, then I suspect that there's a better than 50-50 chance that your company does NOT have an Online Newsroom today. And if I'm correct, don't sweat it. The reality is that it's fairly easy to create an initial Online Newsroom, so let's start with the basics.

At a minimum, I feel there are four items every company needs to start an Online Newsroom. These are

1. Background Materials,
2. News Releases,
3. Media, and
4. PR Contact Information.

Can you have more categories of "things" in your Online Newsroom? Of course, and the larger the enterprise, the greater the likelihood it will have more stuff within its online newsroom. But the reality is that if you have at least these four types of content within your Online Newsroom, you'll be fine.

Before I continue with this RULE, however, I hope you grasp the purpose for having an Online Newsroom in the first place.

The primary goal of an Online Newsroom is simple:

Make it easy for every Journalist to perform his or her job.

That's it.

Can an Online Newsroom do more? Of course.

In fact, I suspect that any prospective employee worth hiring will turn to a company's Online Newsroom to gain a deeper and broader understanding about a firm before even submitting a job application.

Similarly, Online Newsrooms provide a wealth of data and information for prospective investors, partners and others. But since this book is focused on generating positive Publicity results, let's focus there for now.

When it comes to <u>Background Materials</u>, the type of items to consider placing within this section of your Online Newsroom might include

- Facts Sheets (Company and/or Product/Service),
- Backgrounders (Company and/or Product/Service),
- White Papers,
- Industry Overviews,
- Biographies,
- Case Studies,
- Use Cases, and
- More.

The intent of this portion of an Online Newsroom is borne out in its name: Background Materials. In other words, the goal here is to provide background information to Journalists. Nothing more. Nothing less.

The <u>News Release</u> section of an Online Newsroom is even simpler to suss-out. It needs to contain copies of your News Releases.

If you have more than one year's worth of News Releases, then subdivide your releases by year and categorize them in chronological order, with the most recent year placed first in the list. {*NOTE: Do the same thing for the releases within each year too, placing them in reverse chronological order, with releases distributed in December appearing higher on the page than those with a November release date.*}

For example, in an Online Newsroom containing three-plus years' worth of News Releases, you might see something like this:

2016
Apr. 19:	XYZ Company Announces Hiring of New CFO
Mar. 29:	Whiziwhig Sales Exploding for XYZ Company
Mar. 8:	XYZ Company to Hold Open House at its New Warehouse
Feb. 16:	Eight More Ways to Save Time Cleaning Using the New Whiziwhig from XYZ Company
Jan. 19:	XYZ Company Sets Standard for Household Cleaning with its New Whiziwhig
Jan. 19:	Throw Out the Mop, the Broom and the Vacuum Cleaner—The Whiziwhig is Here

2015
2014
2013

So . . . use reverse chronological order, with the latest year at the top of the list, and with the newest release in each year listed first with the oldest release listed last. And (in case it's not clear by the list above), each headline needs to be a hotlink to a copy of the actual News Release found on its own page within your Website.

When it comes to the <u>Media</u> section of your Online Newsroom, I'm referring to visual elements from your company's PR and Marketing storehouse, items such as

- Logos,
- Photographs,
- Charts,
- Tables,
- Videos,
- Etc.

Note that each item included in the <u>Media</u> section of your Online Newsroom should be labeled/titled. Personally, I recommend highlighting the various elements in a thumbnail format within the <u>Media</u> section of Online Newsrooms so Journalists can get an idea of what each item looks like without

1. Having to jump to another page first to see the element in its full size, or
2. Needing to download the item first.

*{**Remember**: The goal of an Online Newsroom is to make a Journalist's life easier, not harder.}*

161

Additionally, I also recommend including both Web-Resolution (72dpi) and High-Resolution (300dpi) versions of each visual element found in your Online Newsroom. For one reason, the smaller Web versions will download a LOT faster than the high-res versions. And for many Journalists, all they'll want/need is a low-resolution image.

On the other hand, having the high-res versions too will ensure that she/he won't have to waste time trying to track you down so you can send them the high-resolution version of that Photo or graphic they need.

Last of all {*and I'm an absolute stickler about this*}, every Online Newsroom must contain <u>PR Contact Information</u> for at least one person from your company who can be reached 24x7x365. In other words, someone at your firm who is available every minute of every single day of every year.

At a minimum, the <u>PR Contact Information</u> for your company should include the

- Name,
- Cell phone number, and
- Email address

of your 24x7x365 PR contact person.

To be clear, this info should be featured prominently on the main page of your Online Newsroom. And (at the risk of overkill) I believe it should also be featured on a separate page within your Online Newsroom.

If you or your 24x7x365 PR contact person have concerns about privacy issues and/or you want to maintain a clear line of demarcation between professional/personal life, gct a separate, PR-only smartphone for this purpose. Then make sure she/he only uses it for PR purposes. But also ensure this PR smartphone is always turned on and always within easy reach.

Now, in reality, do most companies need to be available around-the-clock to support the needs of Journalists? Of course not.

But the bigger or more successful your company, or the more widespread the adoption of your services/products, the greater the likelihood you will have customers outside of your hometown, if not all over the planet. And as soon as you begin Marketing and selling outside of your little corner of the world, you now become fair game for anyone with a Website or Social Media account to write/publish news/information about you, your company and/or your products/services.

And when that happens, you'll want to be ready. Otherwise, you may miss that Publicity opportunity altogether.

Hence, my feelings about 24x7x365 PR contacts.

Beyond the four basic things I feel every Online Newsroom needs to contain —

1. Background Materials,
2. News Releases,
3. Media, and
4. PR Contact Information.

— there are other items you might consider including in your Online Newsroom.

For example, the younger, less established or less well-known your firm is, the more likely you may want to include examples

163

of <u>Stories</u> that have been published about your company or that have featured your company. This can be as simple as highlighting headlines of such <u>Stories</u> and the media outlets that published them (with hotlinks to the actual <u>Stories</u> themselves).

Additionally, some companies' Online Newsrooms include information about <u>Awards</u> they have won, presuming (that is) that a company has actually won <u>Awards</u>.

Other firms include links in an Online Newsroom to their company <u>Blog</u>. Others include links to their most important <u>Social Media</u> accounts or to a section of <u>Customer Testimonials</u>.

But in case there is any question about this, the objective of having and maintaining an Online Newsroom is to produce ***Publicity Success*** for your company. That means you want to make it as easy as possible for any Journalist to produce stories about your firm, your products/services, your customers and you. That's it.

That's also why you need an Online Newsroom.

= = = = = = = = = = = = = = = = = = =

RULE #54: Use Media Alerts Judiciously

If you are planning an event that you want Journalists, Bloggers and/or Industry Analysts to attend, cover or both, then you might want to consider using a Media Alert to attract their interest.

A Media Alert is similar to a News Release in several ways. Specifically, both

- Are designed to announce something,
- Contain factual information about the announcement, and
- Both include contact information for reaching the individual or organization distributing the announcement.

To be useful, a Media Alert needs to contain the following information (at a minimum):

- WHO (or WHAT organization) is announcing WHAT event,
- WHEN the event will be held (including day of the week, date and actual time),
- WHERE the event is going to be held,
- WHY the event announcement is important to WHAT people/organizations, and (if appropriate),
- HOW the upcoming event will affect said people and/or organizations.

To be honest, the layout or design of a Media Alert is less critical than what is included in the Alert itself.

As with any Publicity action, you must be able to objectively determine that the event you are thinking about announcing is, in fact, newsworthy to at least some segment of the population, and therefore to one or more media outlets that "serve" that segment(s). But if you determine that your proposed event is newsworthy, then you're ready to move forward.

Obviously, a Media Alert is of zero use unless it is delivered to the right individuals — Journalists, Bloggers and/or Analysts — in the right timeframe. In some instances, this may mean distributing a Media Alert the day of an event, while in other instances an Alert might be distributed a week or more in advance.

You'll have several options when it comes to getting your Media Alert in front of Journalists, Bloggers and/or Analysts, including

- Hand delivery,
- Postal delivery,
- Overnight Delivery Services,
- Email distribution,
- Social Media postings/updates, or even
- Commercial Wire Services.

Regardless of which delivery mechanism(s) you use, Media Alerts can prove very useful in producing successful events and generating positive media coverage. Examples of some of the Media-Alert-worthy events you might consider are included in RULES 55 and 56 in the pages that follow.

= =

RULE #55: Press Tours, Press Briefings, Press Conferences, Conference Calls and Webcasts: Yes, No or Maybe?

Obviously, each company is different. Some only resell products that other companies make, while other offer services on an international basis. And the simplicity or complexity of the products/services sold can also vary widely from business to business, even within the same industry.

Because the title of this book is 66 RULES for Publicity Success, clearly each RULE is included herein because I believe that there is at least the potential of generating positive media coverage by properly executing the RULE in question.

And that is the case for this RULE — with one primary caveat . . . it depends.

"It depends upon what," you ask? Actually, a whole lot of factors.

Such factors start with determining the honest-to-goodness newsworthiness of the announcement you are planning to make. But additional factors can also include

- Your industry,
- Your competitors,
- Your products/services,
- Your executives,
- The time of day,
- The day of the week,
- The month,
- The season,
- External events you have zero control over,

- External people you have zero control over,
- Your own employees,
- Local government actions/inactions,
- State government actions/inactions,
- Federal government actions/inactions,
- Rulings by the judiciary,
- Acts of war,
- Terrorist attacks,
- Acts of God/Nature, and
- On and on and on.

For example, as a way of prefacing the hoped for and even anticipated success of any Publicity undertaking, I have long told both clients and employers the following (or something akin to this):

Even if we do everything perfectly, if 1) the Pope dies, or 2) lunatics decide to fly airliners into skyscrapers, or 3) a natural disaster kills thousands of people, all bets are off when it comes to successfully generating the desired Publicity results.

Is that statement above politically correct? Absolutely not. Is it accurate? No question about it.

So . . . should you include

- Press Tours,
- Press Briefings,
- Press Conferences,
- Conference Calls, and
- Webcasts

in your bag of Publicity tools for your company? Maybe.

Each can generate gangbuster results. But you first need to objectively consider how newsworthy the announcement is you are planning to make vis-à-vis the 20 or so considerations listed on the previous pages.

If you can honestly say to yourself, "Yup, I've got a real opportunity on my hands," then great. Now you're ready for the next consideration:

What's the best vehicle for generating the best possible
Publicity outcome given all of the variables at hand?

In today's hyper-connected and interactive world, there's truly something to be said for conducting one-on-one or one-to-many Webcasts, especially when it comes to eliminating travel costs and compressing timeframes for getting the word out to as many people as possible within the shortest time possible.

Then again (depending upon the news you have to share), the best approach may be actually getting on the road and sitting down face-to-face with Journalists where they work as part of a Press Tour. This can be especially true if your efforts surround a physical product and/or if personal interaction can improve the outcome of what some professionals term "Desk-Side Briefings."

Realistically, without knowing all of the different variables you and your company face today, I cannot offer a blanket statement that one Publicity activity will always be successful versus another for your company — especially those listed in this RULE. Only you can make that determination.

But I can tell you this: Each of the Publicity tactics listed in this RULE can work. That I do know.

= =

RULE #56: Press Receptions — Yes, No or Maybe?

There are two types of Press Receptions:

- Those produced by a third party for the benefit of other companies, and
- A self-produced Press Reception.

Let's consider both in turn.

Press Receptions Produced by Third Parties:

In the consumer electronics, computer and technology worlds, there are a dozen or more Press Receptions produced each year by third parties in the U.S., with the main receptions being produced by two companies:

- Showstoppers (www.showstoppers.com), and
- PEPCOM (www.pepcom.com).

Both of these companies produce fantastic Press Receptions, which (in plain English) are

Events lasting several hours that are co-sponsored by companies as a way to highlight their wares in front of lots of Journalists, Bloggers, Analysts and investors at one time.

Think of Press Receptions as miniature trade shows held exclusively for Journalists, Bloggers, Analysts and investors (aka, money people).

Here's how they work.

The producers rent out an area for a Press Reception, typically a large ballroom or hall in a major resort hotel/casino. They then outfit the hall with the requisite fixings, such as Internet connections (wired and wireless), skirted folding tables, chairs, signage, food stations, bars, cocktail tables and the like. Outside the hall, the producers set up elaborate check-in/registration stations, with the requisite security professionals to ensure that only credentialed individuals are admitted to each event.

Companies prep their assigned display stations inside the ballroom/hall, sometimes hours in advance, with the hopes of attracting and snaring on-the-fly briefings with numerous Journalists about their latest and greatest offerings.

Then (at the appointed hour), the doors open, credentialed Journalists, Bloggers, Analysts and investors stream inside, with some heading directly for one of the strategically placed bars and/or food stations, while others begin the process of looking for that next big scoop or opportunity. And then for the next three to four hours it's a mad house as employees, in-house publicists, consultants, and PR agency representatives pursue the highest profile journos and story opportunities they can.

The largest third-party, independently produced Press Receptions in the U.S. are conducted in early January during the International CES trade show — that crazy tech-fest celebrating consumer electronics that nearly crushes Las Vegas, Nevada each year.

{NOTE: For example, the 2016 CES attracted over 170,000 attendees from all over the world, as well as over 6,000 Journalists of all stripes.}

The largest independently produced Press Reception my employer co-sponsored under my direction had 125-plus companies as co-sponsors and attracted over 1,000 Journalists, Bloggers, Analysts and investors for a four-hour event.

My results at that particular event? Over 100 briefings within four hours. Yeah, it was absolutely insane! Then again, it was absolutely worth it!

Self-Produced Press Receptions:

From my perspective, a Press Reception produced by a company for itself is very similar to a Press Conference with one major exception —

> *A Self-Produced Press Reception is a Press Conference that turns into a celebration/party.*

And to be clear, I don't think there is anything wrong with having a celebration/party. But let's be transparent on what such an event is and what it is not.

Specifically, a Press Conference is a fairly straightforward affair:

- A company holds an event to make one announcement or more to multiple media outlets at one time.

- Unless tied to a crisis event, Press Conferences are typically held during the day, generally in the morning prior to noon newscasts.
- Food and non-alcoholic beverages may be served, but they are NOT required.
- The general announcement is made to all media members at the same time.
- Publicity materials about the announcement(s) are distributed on-site to Journalists in attendance.
- One-on-one post-announcement briefings are available for interested Journalists/media outlets.
- The entire event is wrapped up within a relatively short period of time, typically one hour or less.

Although a Press Conference has many similarities with a Self-Produced Press Reception, there are exceptions. For example, a Self-Produced Press Reception will often

- Be held outside of normal business hours, generally at night.
- Be more of an elaborate affair than a Press Conference and will often include the serving of alcoholic drinks.
- Include company employees outside the communications or Marketing departments, as well as non-executives. It's also possible that spouses, significant others, family members and even non-employees will attend, and people such as customers, partners, investors and others may be invited to attend, too.

- Take more of a miniature-tradeshow approach, with multiple product/service stations setup within the event location.
- Have more of a festive flair.
- Last much longer than one hour.
- Tend to be more focused on generating local news coverage, unless the event is held
    - In a major media center, like New York City, Los Angeles, San Francisco or other metropolitan centers with a large population of media outlets focused on international, national or trade media topics, or is held
    - During (or in conjunction with) a significant industry event, such as a trade show, conference or exposition that attracts Journalists from outside the geographical area.

Which Is Better — Independent Third-Party Produced or Self-Produced Press Receptions?

To be clear, both Independently Produced and Self-Produced Press Receptions have value, and both can be very beneficial in successfully generating Publicity for your company.

However, I believe that typically only companies with larger budgets, staffs and/or consultants can successfully pull off a Self-Produced Press Reception.

Conversely, for relatively low, out-of-pocket-costs — *sub-$5,000 in some instances* — any company of any size can participate in an Independently Produced Press

Reception and have the chance to attract the attention of hundreds of Journalists, Bloggers, Analysts and investors in one multi-hour event. And on top of that, all you have to do is show up with Publicity materials and products in hand, and you must be ready to pitch your story over and over again at an Independently Produced Press Reception.

By contrast, with a Self-Produced Press Reception you also have to take care of (and pay for) all of the ancillary planning, setup, execution and tear-down of the event itself. To me, that additional effort is typically too much work for the incremental benefits (if any) of conducting a Self-Produced Press Reception.

In other words, I believe it's typically NOT worth it for most organizations to put on their own event. But then again, it CAN be worth it — you just have to run a cost-benefit analysis *in advance* to make the proper determination.

= = = = = = = = = = = = = = = = = = = =

RULE #57: Private Groups in Social Media — Yes, No or Maybe?

Should you create "Private Groups" in Social Media platforms? To me the answer is a qualified "yes." Here's why.

There are primarily two Social Media platforms in the U.S. today where individuals and organizations can create Private Groups:

- *LinkedIn*, and
- *Facebook*.

Both platforms have enormous potential for delivering great value to organizations that create/maintain Private Groups on them. But let's be very clear about the primary distinctions between these two platforms —

- *LinkedIn* is almost exclusively used for professional purposes, while
- *Facebook* is used for both personal and professional purposes.

Clearly there are exceptions to these purposes, but if you market/sell products/services primarily to consumers, you almost certainly want to use *Facebook* for Private (or "Closed") Groups. Conversely, if you have services/products that are primarily targeted at professional end-users, *LinkedIn* is often going to be your best bet for Private Groups.

{NOTE: Notwithstanding the opinion in the prior paragraph, Facebook is clearly a lot larger than LinkedIn (based upon the number of users— 1.6 billion vs. 400 million, respectively). As a result, numerous organizations HAVE turned to FB for their Private Groups. Thought you should know.}

Once you understand these distinctions, however, then the next question you must address is this:

> *If you setup a Private/Closed Group, will you dedicate the necessary resources to the Group to maintain it over time?*

If your answer to this question is "no," then you should NOT setup a Private Group on ANY Social Media platform because you will likely cause more harm to your organization than good.

If, however, your answer is "yes" — *you commit in advance to dedicate the resources to such a Private Group and to maintain/support that Private Group over time* — then maybe you should proceed forward.

Just recognize that any Private Group will require a lot of time, and for most people (and organizations), that will be the most precious resource required.

= = = = = = = = = = = = = = = = = = = =

SECTION 9: MISCELLANEOUS

Within this section you will find nine additional RULES (and one BONUS RULE) that don't truly fit in to any of the previous sections, but that nonetheless deserve to be included within the pages of 66 RULES for Publicity Success. I hope you agree.

= = = = = = = = = = = = = = = = = = =

RULE #58: Become an Expert

If you want to achieve ***Publicity Success***, then you need to "become" an expert in your particular field of choice.

> {*NOTE: When I use the words "you" or "your" in this RULE, the advice also applies to positioning your boss, colleague or client as an expert too.*}

If you are selling/marketing products or services with any degree of accomplishment, chances are you have at least some level of "expert-ness" or expertise. The challenge, however, often comes from getting Journalists to

1. Know that you exist, and
2. Accept you as a reliable resource.

Identifying the right media outlets and the right Journalists are key to leveraging your "expert-ness" into positive media coverage.

Such media outlets can range from a hometown paper (like the *Waco Tribune-Herald*) to a major TV station like *WABC*, or from an industry newsletter (such as *Dentistry Today*) to a major magazine (like *Fortune*).

But if you can target the right outlet and the right Journalist(s), you may be well on your way to Expert Heaven!

{*NOTE: Don't forget to take advantage of **Publicity 3.0** tactics by publishing your expert ideas and commentaries on media properties you own and/or lease/rent. Such efforts will help you to communicate directly with current (and prospective) customers, employees, investors, partners and more.*}

= =

RULE #59: Give Speeches & Deliver Presentations

I was not quite five years into my career, working as a Senior Account Executive at TFB/Davis in Seattle, when I had my first experience with the Publicity benefits of giving a speech.

My then boss, Peter Horan, landed a slot to speak at the monthly meeting of the Seattle chapter of the National Venture Capital Association (NVCA). So (as the head PR dude at our agency), I made sure we

- Prepped and distributed a Media Alert pre-announcing Peter's speech,
- Pitched the topic of Peter's speech to one or two business Journalists in the area, and
- Summarized the key points from his speech in a post-event News Release we distributed to the Journalists after-the-fact.

And (sure enough), the local weekly business paper ran a story about Peter's speech in the next edition.

A few years later, my former agency — Politis Communications — was able to transform a 10-minute presentation of a scientific abstract at the annual meeting of the American Chemical Society (ACS) into over 200 written articles published within a six-week period, including three separate stories written by one reporter with the *Associated Press*, as well as a report that was broadcast numerous times across a 60-station radio network.

{***NOTE****: This was before the advent of the World Wide Web and online digital publishing, so 200 stories was actually was a pretty big deal.* }

My point is this . . . giving speeches and delivering presentations are great vehicles for

- Positioning yourself (or your boss or client) as an expert on a given subject, and
- Generating positive media coverage for you, your company and your products/services.

Being successful within this arena merely requires a little forethought, some advance preparation and a bit of follow-up after-the-fact (as outlined above).

And (as outlined in RULE #58), don't forget to self-promote such speeches/presentations via the media properties you own, rent or lease.

= =

RULE #60: Become an Author — Specifically a Self-Published Author

According to hedge fund manager, serial entrepreneur and *Wall Street Journal* bestselling author James Altucher,

> *If you . . . self-publish a book you will stand out, you will make more money, you will kick your competitors right in the XX, and you will look amazingly cool at cocktail parties.*

You know what? He's right.

In case you didn't know, I was a self-syndicated columnist for roughly 10 years, between 1993 and 2003.

> {***NOTE***: *Officially, my column* Utah Tech Watch *started out as a biweekly column carried by* The Daily Herald *[in Provo, Utah] for six months, before moving to weekly status at the* Herald. *Then it was picked up a few months later by the* Deseret News; *within a year of starting my column,* The Enterprise *[in Salt Lake City] also picked up my column.*}

Becoming a self-syndicated columnist writing about a topic I knew well — the technology world — did more good for me professionally, and for my business, than any other one Marketing effort I had ever undertaken previously.

How? Simply put, not too long after my column switched to weekly status, I reached out to several broadcast Producers and print business Editors/Reporters in the area to let them know if they ever needed an "expert" to help

- Explain a certain technology problem or
- Discuss a technology topic

for their viewers, listeners or readers, I was happy to do so. And then I did.

During the 10-plus years I wrote *Utah Tech Watch* I was interviewed for tech stories by various mainstream media outlets probably 150-200 times. And even today, some 10-plus years since my last column ran, I still get the occasional call asking if I can provide insights into various tech topics.

Clearly, writing a column is not the same thing as writing and self-publishing a book. But I'm confident there are enough similarities that I can make this claim here.

In truth, I could probably dedicate an entire book to covering the benefits of self-publishing a book. But I don't need to do this as there are already dozens of books written about the Hows, Whys and Benefits of self-publishing — including the Publicity benefits of becoming an author.

And although I can't attest to the quality of these authors' writing skills or their particular counsel, they're also right.

That's why one of my 66 RULES for achieving ***Publicity Success*** is to

Become an Author — Specifically a Self-Published Author.

= = = = = = = = = = = = = = = = = = =

RULE #61: Give Back to Society

Altruistically, it would be wonderful if every person and every business were philanthropic in nature — if charity not only began at home but expanded to include the halls of businesses everywhere.

It turns out that there is a growing contingent of commercial enterprises that do, in fact, give back to society. And I'm referring to more than just firms involved in the outdoor industry, socially responsible entities, or the relatively new invention known as "B Corporations."

But not everyone is wired to think or act charitably, especially in a business setting. And to be honest, I believe that the primary purpose of business is quite simple:

to generate profits by providing products/services that customers buy.

In my perspective, profit-making is NOT a bad or evil thing {*despite what some people might say*}.

There is, however, a real upside for business owners and smart companies of all sizes to give back to society, or at least some aspect of society.

For the record, this RULE is not centered on the concept of Corporate Sponsorship:

> *Payment in cash (or other resources) in order to have its name/product/services associated with another organization.*

The most visible of such sponsorships are found within sports and athletics. Examples range from the almost prosaic, like the

Little League Baseball team named after the local bank, to the extraordinary, such as the naming of a stadium or arena, like Citi Field or the mouthful that is now known as the Vivint Smart Home Arena, respectively. And to be clear, I am not opposed whatsoever to Corporate Sponsorships per se, such as buying *Corporate Naming Rights*, as long as such sponsorships are in line with the overall Marketing goals and objectives of the organization.

Rather, I'm thinking more along the ways that organizations can truly "give back to society." Such "giving back" can be in the form of financial donations to support various causes, such as supporting homeless shelters, breast cancer awareness, or providing clean drinking water to those who do not have the benefit of such a luxury.

Other companies allow their employees to spend a certain amount of time each month donating service to a charitable cause, time off that is paid for by the employers. Another way to give back is by volunteering to serve a community and/or non-profit organization.

Personally, this is the path I have taken during my career — opportunities where I have followed the concept purportedly espoused by Benjamin Franklin, that of

"Doing well by doing good."

In other words, in volunteering I have done so knowing in advance that by offering my time and my skills to causes I support (typically professional business organizations), my service would

- Benefit others, but would also
- Introduce me to other like-minded professionals —
  individuals potentially in positions where they could
  - Hire me, or
  - Recommend me to others.

To be honest, it is a great feeling to recognize that I was put in a position to potentially win someone's business because I gave back to the community.

But then again, there is often a deep feeling of contentment that I "won" specifically because I had helped out something or someone that I believed in. Now ***THAT*** is satisfying.

Satisfaction alone, however, will not generate ***Publicity Success*** for you or your business. This is where a lot of companies fall short in maximizing the potential benefits that can be derived from giving back to society.

To be clear, savvy executives also understand that it is possible to go over the line in attempting to garner too much media coverage for the charitable acts and/or donations of their organizations. Case in point, distributing News Releases or holding Press Conferences every time a company makes a $1,000 donation to a worthy cause will diminish the credibility of both the donor and the recipient. {***FYI***: *I can just imagine the eye-roll of an Editor at* The Atlanta Constitution-Journal *as she receives another donation News Release and thinks, "Another stupid announcement from XYZ Company. Duh!"*}

However, this is where the role of **Publicity 3.0** tools, tactics and strategies can come into play to the benefit of an organization and its efforts to achieve ***Publicity Success***.

186

For example, if your company is supporting a charitable cause by allowing/encouraging executives/employees to donate their time to such an organization, you should use your Social Media accounts to publicize your support for that cause and/or non-profit. This can be done on the Web via written Updates, uploaded Photos or Videos, or even Blog posts praising your employees/execs for their support of the worthy cause(s).

Additionally, although a financial donation might not be significant enough to warrant a standalone News Release, per sé, that doesn't prevent you from producing an oversized check, taking a Photo of you handing the oversized check to an executive at the charity, and sharing that Photo on one or more of your Social Media accounts, right? And at the same time, you should also heap praise on the charitable cause and all the good it does in the world.

Naturally, if your firm is a HUGE supporter of a particular cause and/or charity, then you should probably write about it as well on your company Blog. {*And on your personal Blog too, if you have one.*}

In the end, as you implement a **Publicity 3.0** approach to giving back to society, you can also reap the rewards of your charitable support without being a lout or appearing to be holier-than-thou. And this is another example of how you can achieve a higher level of ***Publicity Success*** through giving back to society.

= =

RULE #62: Go Where They Are *(Trade Shows, Conferences & Exhibitions)*

If you're not doing so already, you should meet with Journalists, Analysts and Bloggers at trade shows, conferences and exhibitions.

The larger the event, the more likely Journalists are to be on hand. That spells an opportunity for you to conduct both pre-scheduled and impromptu media interviews and briefings at your booth.

I've found there are always news professionals willing to meet at shows/events if you will

- Take the time to craft/prepare your story idea(s) in advance, and
- Make the effort to *reach out to Journalists in a timely and appropriate manner.*

At some of the smaller shows I have attended in the past, such efforts have landed only a handful of meetings with members of the media, but that was okay as such results were in line with my expectations.

Conversely, at some of the largest trade shows, I have had some instances where I have held interviews and briefings with more than 100 Bloggers, Reporters, Editors, Reviewers and Analysts during one event. Regardless of your industry or your business's stage of life, you should always look for opportunities to meet with members of the media while you're at exhibitions, conferences, trade shows and other such events.

= =

RULE #63: Spellcheck AND Proofread

Should you use a spellchecker? Absolutely. Is it enough? Absolutely not!

Anytime you write or edit a new document, you need to **check your spelling**. In this regard, the spellchecker features of many leading software applications do a wonderful job . . . as far as as they go.

Unfortunately, not all spellcheckers include grammar functionality. As a result, you might correctly spell the word "their" when you really meant to use the word "there" or "they're" —which (you may know) are homynyms of each other; in other words, they sound the same, but have different spellings and meanings.

Or you might make the near job-ending mistake I made in my first year as a public relations professional and type the term "*pubic* relations" when I intended to write "*public* relations." Yes, I left out the letter "L" out of the word "public." And yes, I got teased mercilessly for my mistake.

That's why spellchecking alone is insufficient: **you must also proofread everything intended for public consumption**, even if you only have one other person as the intended audience (such as in a private email).

Good proofreading will catch most of the mistakes that a spellcheck program will not. That's why you need to do both. In most instances you'll continue to proofread the way you always have — by starting at the beginning of a document, reading through to the end and making edits as you go.

= = = = = = = = = = = = = = = = = = = =

BONUS RULE: Read Backward

One additional idea to consider, however, is to proofread documents by reading backwards. In other words, you should begin at the end of a document and read from the the bottom of the page up to the top of the page while reading from right to left.

*I'll tell you in advance that this process **is** laborious.*

However, your brain will not automatically glide over tricky mistakes that standard proofreading will miss — like someone who has accidentally typed the word "the" consecutively in a sentence. {For example, did you catch that exact "mistake" in the first paragraph of this BONUS RULE?}

*If you didn't, don't feel bad — most people will miss that mistake when reading or proofreading the "normal way." But if you **proofread documents backward**, you'll catch such mistakes nearly every time.*

= = = = = = = = = = = = = = = = = = = =

RULE #64: Tell the Truth

While reading an article this morning, I was reminded about a basic underlying principle of public relations that seems so obvious that I almost wasn't going to include it as one of the RULES of this book. But then I decided to anyway.

That principle is this:

Tell the truth.

If you ever want to undo all of the goodwill and positive vibes you have generated for your company, client, products, services or people, just lie. In fact, lie in such a way so as to ensure you will get caught red-handed, and do so in a way that those who catch you will be the very Journalists who are covering your company and industry.

Not sure who or what I'm talking about? Here's an example:

Do a little digging into the U.S. Presidential candidacy of Senator Gary Hart, especially his 1987-1988 presidential run. What you'll find (if you didn't know it already) is that Senator Hart's campaign was undone after he claimed there was no truth to rumors he was involved in an extramarital relationship and challenged Journalists to "follow him around," but then he warned that they'd "be very bored" if they did so.

Turns out he was wrong.

Based upon an anonymous tip, the *Miami Herald* followed Hart-campaign staffer Donna Rice from Miami to Hart's Washington, D.C. townhouse where she allegedly spent the entire evening — an "overnighter" the *Herald* gleefully reported on.

Interestingly, a few months after Hart withdrew from the race, the celebrity tabloid *National Enquirer* ran a Photo showing Rice and Hart holding hands and smiling at the camera, with Hart wearing a "Monkey Business Crew" t-shirt and Rice sitting on Hart's lap.

Now . . . do I know for a fact that Senator Hart lied to the media about his relationship with Rice and/or other women? No, I do not.

But I do know this: Public perception that Hart had lied killed his quest to become the President of the United States of America.

For the record . . . becoming a liar, either as an individual or as an organization, will dramatically undercut your credibility and your ability to be successful, both now and in the future.

So . . . if that's what you're looking for, if that's what you want to achieve, you go ahead: Share those falsehoods with Journalists, publish those deceiving statements, distribute News Releases that include intentional untruths. Go right ahead. Knock yourself out.

Me? I'm gonna tell the truth.

That's what I advise everyone else to do as well.

= =

RULE #65: Eschew Obfuscation

Eschew obfuscation? *Absolutely!*

In case you're a bit murky on the phrase, *Dictionary.com* defines these words thusly:

- es-**choo**: to abstain or keep away from; shun; avoid
- **ob**-*fuh*-skey-shun: to confuse, bewilder or stupefy; to make obscure or unclear

In other words, **avoid** making things confusing, bewildering or unclear.

Said in Plain English, K-I-S-S: Keep It Simple, Stupid.

This is what I always try to do when I talk about the concept of *The Betty Factor* back in RULE #1.

Everything you write, speak, show or communicate through any media or in any venue should be clear enough that your 80-something-year-old mother-in-law can understand it. For me, that's *Betty.*

If *Betty* doesn't understand what you're trying to communicate, then you've failed. Go back to the drawing board and try again. And keep trying until your "*Betty*" gets it.

Once she does . . . BINGO, you can move forward.

In the meantime, *eschew obfuscation!*

= = = = = = = = = = = = = = = = = = =

RULE #66: Be Prepared — Create a Crisis Communications Plan

The cliché suggests it's like "watching a wreck in slow motion." And you know what? The cliché is correct.

For this RULE, I thought it might be helpful to share a real-world example of the process I went through several years ago as my agency prepped for the coming media and business storm caused by a client's primary competitor and business friend: a *"Frenemy,"* if you will.

Here's what happened:

One of my clients, a regional computer dealer named PC Laptops, was anticipating the self-destruction of one of its very visible (yet friendly) competitors, a company known as Totally Awesome Computers. However, the fact that Totally Awesome was led by an individual whose antics had made him a lightning rod for media coverage and criticism made this expected implosion dicey at best.

As it became clear that Totally Awesome was, in fact, going to self-destruct, our challenges in a crisis communications sense became clear.

> <u>One:</u> How could my agency help PC Laptops stay clear of the blast zone created by its competitor's self-detonation and not be damaged perception-wise in the process?

> <u>Two:</u> And potentially more importantly, what steps could be taken (if any) to create a beneficial outcome for our client from the anticipated fall of Totally Awesome?

So what did we do? Here's a brief overview of the efforts we took that you might find useful as a crisis communications checklist.

CRISIS COMMUNICATIONS CHECKLIST

1.   You don't know what you don't know.

One of the biggest challenges in any crisis is speed. Things often happen so fast and decisions need to be made so quickly, that the risk is that any communications misstep along the way can prove disastrous. Hence, it's imperative that you do as much research and planning in advance as possible.

In this case, our research showed us a couple of things.

- Both PC Laptops and Totally Awesome Computers had huge name recognition already, with a mostly negative bent toward the competitor and mostly positive to ambivalent feelings toward our client.
- We were also able to uncover the most likely scenario for the shuttering of Totally Awesome.

2.   Assume the worst in your planning.

In an idyllic world, all of our worries and fretting would come to naught and the sun would set in a rosy hue of pink every evening. However, in the real world, people lie and cheat and steal and the unexpected happens a lot more often than most of us would like to think. Therefore, when it comes to *creating a Crisis Communications Plan*, you have to assume the worst and plan accordingly.

195

We had hoped that our client would be able to communicate with the media (and thus its customers) in a controlled environment without any interference from Totally Awesome Computers.

However, we also realized this was probably not likely given the media-hungry nature of the competitor's founder/owner and his propensity for verbal self-flagellation in front of the news media. We also agreed that it was likely that information about the closing of Totally Awesome's business would be leaked to the media and that some (or all of this leakage) would contain at least some false or inaccurate information.

So we planned accordingly. And (as it turns out) we were correct in each of these assumptions.

For better or worse, Totally Awesome Computers did not successfully manage the closing of its business in a controlled manner. Hence, customers who showed up on the fateful morning at several Totally Awesome locations found hand-written signs taped to their front doors stating the company was out of business. And yet other Totally Awesome locations remained inexplicitly open on the same day.

I won't go over all the details surrounding this crisis situation or our planning prior to Totally Awesome's shutdown. However, within 96 hours PC Laptops had

- Expanded to eight locations from six locations,
- Conducted over 100 job interviews and hired nearly 30 new highly qualified sales and technical professionals, and
- Generated dramatically positive media coverage, all while

- Significantly distancing itself from its now-defunct competitor and its mercurial owner/operator.

And I would suggest that a large portion of that success came from crafting and following a *Crisis Communications Plan*.

= =

CONCLUSION

As I come to the end of this writing journey, the 2016 presidential election cycle is in full swing here in the United States. And Journalists of all types seem to be falling all over themselves as they report that "Donald Trump said this" or "Hillary Clinton did that," while political prognosticators opine on the meaning behind the results of one poll versus those of another.

As a Public Relations professional with over 30 years under his belt, watching this recurrent, four-year cycle unfold is like being a choc-a-holic with a free, all-you-can-eat pass to visit a Hershey's chocolate factory. In other words: *I can't get enough of it.* Then again, I also understand that times like these can feel overwhelming for business owners trying to stand out from the crowd with a successful Publicity program.

And yet, during my morning readings earlier today I learned about 10-plus local businesses I didn't even know existed, all because they were highlighted in *Draper Lifestyle*, the monthly magazine published in the city where I live. Additionally, I saw products from several companies featured in the pages of a recent *Inc.* magazine issue, one of which — Moleskin — makes my favorite notebook for capturing ideas on paper. And just this past week while out of town for a conference, I caught a short story on a national news channel about several entrepreneurs being featured for their successful business efforts.

"But what about me?" you may be thinking. "I'm not a celebrity, and my company is not well known. Why would any media outlet want to do a story about me?"

Trust me; I understand such sentiments. But just because your last name isn't Kardashian or your company isn't named Uber or Wal-Mart, don't allow yourself to be fooled into falsely believing that you cannot achieve ***Publicity Success***.

Why? Because it's not true!

The reality is that any company, including yours, has the ability to capture new customers, drive more sales, expand into new markets, and grow in value as you learn and apply the 66 RULES for Publicity Success found within these pages.

This means comprehending the purpose and value of *The Betty Factor*, as well as producing an Elevator Pitch and other PR materials that ideally position your products/services against competitors so customers recognize the benefits you provide to the marketplace.

Hopefully, by this point in this book you've also grasped the role Journalists fill in filtering, aggregating and delivering news and information to the target audiences they serve. More importantly, you now understand some of the most critical tools and vehicles at your disposal for communicating your news, information and stories to achieve ***Publicity Success*** with media coverage that can transform your marketplace — including the concept of content creation and self-publishing for wins in the media coverage game via **Publicity 3.0** strategies and tactics.

At its best, ***Publicity Success*** means taking individuals from where they know nothing about you, your company or your goods/services to where they become rabid fans, committed customers who help you sell your goods and services and grow your company — *as well as increase its value* — beyond anything you have previously known. And from my perspective, any business owner can achieve such success.

Case in point, I offer the story of Rubicon Medical.

= =

CASE STUDY: *From Pennies to Millions*

I was introduced to Rubicon Medical by an investor in the company who also happened to be a long-time business associate of mine, someone who told me Rubicon needed my help.

An early stage medical device company, Rubicon Medical had invented a parachute-like contraption that was shaped somewhat like a witch's hat. This device was made from a material that allowed cardiologists to simply and quickly remove deadly plaque during stenting procedures as they opened clogged arteries. It was a novel approach to a tricky problem, one that had not yet been cleared by the United States Food & Drug Administration or any other regulatory body around the globe, but one that showed promise in early animal testing.

The challenge was this: To stay alive financially, Rubicon had been forced to raise money via a reverse shell merger, a transaction that infused some capital into Rubicon while the firm became a publicly traded company overnight. Unfortunately, the reverse merger was orchestrated by "pump & dump" specialists who artificially jacked-up the per share price to roughly $1.25 before bailing out of the stock. As a result, the day I met Rubicon's CEO, the company's share price was at 35 cents per share and headed downward where it would soon bottom out at seven cents per share three months later.

200

66 RULES for Publicity Success

"Stop wasting your time on Investor Relations," I told the CEO. "Brokers can't recommend your stock because it's trading at under five bucks a share. But . . . you have a great story to tell; let's tell it."

And so we began the process to do just that — to achieve **Publicity Success** *for Rubicon Medical.*

Less than two months later we had landed a positive write-up about Rubicon and its dime-sized Rubicon Filter in The Enterprise, *a small, weekly newspaper in Salt Lake City that focused on the business community. Shortly thereafter, Rubicon's stock (listed on the Over-the-Counter Bulletin Board system under the symbol RMDC) began to turn around.*

As we continued our media relations program for Rubicon, we focused on defining and describing the widespread problems the Rubicon Filter addressed. With millions of people suffering with plaque-clogged blood vessels, the use of expandable wire-mesh stents to open those vessels created follow-on, secondary risk from downstream blockages caused by plaque that could break free and lead to kidney failure, stroke or even death. Thus, the need for the Rubicon Filter.

Within nine months of beginning our media relations campaign, RMDC had rebounded from 7¢/share to over 50¢/share. More importantly, Rubicon's work in "embolic filtration" (the technical term for the focus of the Rubicon Filter — filtering potentially deadly gunk known as emboli from a bloodstream after a stenting event) had attracted the attention of medical device giant Boston Scientific, which invested $2 million into Rubicon Medical. Several months later, Boston Scientific invested an additional $15 million in Rubicon, gaining a total 18% stake in the Salt Lake City-based firm, along with an option to acquire the balance of the company at a future date.

In the end, roughly 30 months after beginning our Publicity program for Rubicon and after the company received total combined cash investments of $17 million, Boston Scientific exercised its option to purchase Rubicon at a potential buyout total of nearly $200 million — an increase of almost 50 times. Clearly, our Publicity campaign was not the only reason why Rubicon and its shareholders saw such a dramatic increase in value in two-and-a-half years. Obviously, the Rubicon team had identified a huge hole in the device marketplace and had aggressively pursued that opportunity.

But make no mistake about it: **Publicity Success** *for Rubicon Medical translated into a HUGE UPSIDE for its investors within a very short time frame, a message clearly delivered by Rubicon Co-Founder and CEO, Richard J. Linder:*

"Four months after hiring Politis Communications our stock price began to turn around, and by the end of the year we had $17 million in new capital and a firm option to sell the company."

= = = = = = = = = = = = = = = = = = = =

Naturally, each circumstance is different, as is every company and each line of products and/or services that it offers. Nevertheless, I do believe this:

You have a greater shot of achieving <u>Business Success</u> *through a targeted Publicity program versus any other Marketing program.*

66 RULES for Publicity Success

And by ***Business Success*** I mean driving action with your targeted publics and increasing the overall value of your firm.

Why do I feel this way? Because when a Journalist tells us that the products from XYZ Company are better than competing products, we tend to believe them. This fact especially holds true in America, the land where *freedom of the press* was born.

Although "the media" is not as sacrosanct or infallible as it once was, the reality is that Journalists still carry a lot of credibility and tend to be given the benefit of the doubt more so than not. Interestingly, Americans lend similar credence to online Journalists as well, even if their only channel for disseminating news, information and/or opinion is via a Social Media platform, such as *YouTube* or *Twitter*.

So . . . if you haven't started implementing the RULES found within the pages of this book, please get started — now!

Even a basic Publicity program will lead to greater visibility in the marketplace and increased credibility for you, your firm and your products/services. A Publicity program will also help you to generate new leads, increase sales, improve your bottom line and more . . . even if initially all you can muster is a **Publicity 3.0** campaign centered around media coverage that YOU produce via self-publishing efforts. The bottom line is that **any** Publicity program can help make your business more successful.

Will starting a Publicity campaign transform your company into a buyout candidate that sees its perceived value rocket skyward 50 times in less than three years?

Probably not. But it might, and that's the point.

66 RULES for Publicity Success

At the end of the day the objective of 66 RULES for Publicity Success is to help you achieve the goals and objectives ***you have set*** for your business. Not me.

Depending upon your business that might mean landing a few new clients or bringing home a few thousand dollars in additional profit each month. And if either of those outcomes can occur for you, GREAT! Go for it!

Conversely, you might be trying to completely revolutionize an entire industry, in which case you may need to raise millions and millions of dollars to help you achieve your dream. If that's the case, cool! A targeted Publicity program is probably exactly what you need.

Regardless, you define your business goals and objectives as you choose to define them. Not me.

But when it comes to achieving those goals and objectives, I'm confident that the concepts — *nope, the RULES* — outlined within 66 RULES for Publicity Success will help you get there faster and less expensively than any other Marketing program you may try.

So get started — *today*. Better yet, start now!

= =

EPILOGUE

The Tired Tinkerer

A faint breeze filtered through the upper portion of the twice-repaired screen door, creating miniature swirls of dust in the front room of the Tompson home as Robert watched Vanna White reveal three As on the puzzle board. He was waiting on supper; meanwhile, the puzzle displayed the name of a place containing five words, and 11 of the 24 letters had already been uncovered:

$$TH\_ \ \_N\_T\_D \ \_TAT\_\_ \ \_\_ \ A\_\_\_\_CA$$

"C'mon," Robert thought. "The United States of America. The United States of America."

It was like he was trying to will the middle-aged construction worker to hear his thoughts all the way from the walls of their 37-year-old home, even though the show was taped two weeks earlier, a fact that Robert clearly didn't know as Pat Sajak turned and asked the contestant if he would like to solve the puzzle.

"Nope," he said as he reached for the Wheel to give it another spin.

Moments later, their Golden Retriever stirred in his familiar spot in front of the TV, lifting and cocking his head toward the front porch.

"What is it, Buster?"

He hadn't heard anything himself, not that that was surprising given he had left his hearing aids next to the bathroom sink when he'd washed his hands for supper. But Robert had learned to trust his canine pal of 11 years, so he began the laborious process of getting out of his recliner to head to the front door.

66 RULES for Publicity Success

He arrived just in time to see a young-ish stranger pause before he took the first of two steps up to their porch. He had a neatly trimmed yet full auburn beard, with aviator-style sunglasses perched on top of a precisely coifed head of slightly darker hair. And although he was wearing a red, black and white plaid work shirt and dark cerulean blue jeans, they clearly hadn't been purchased anyplace within 500 miles of Dubuque, a fact confirmed by the $500 brown loafers the man was wearing.

"Can I help you, son?" Robert asked, startling the unexpected visitor.

He glanced up, definitely surprised as he began fumbling for something in his breast pocket.

"I'm sorry, sir," he began as he stepped forward up the stairs, business card extended out to the gray-haired man in front of him. "I would have called first, but I couldn't find the right number. By any chance are you Robert Tompson?"

Robert swung the screen door wide with one arm as he reached for the proffered card.

"That would be me," Robert replied as he read New Century Ventures *across the top of the card. It was thick, thicker than typical business cards.*

"And?" he asked expectantly.

"I'm Tommy Aaron," the stranger answered. "And I've come a long way to meet you, Mr. Tompson. I'm here because I read about your invention on the Internet. Could I have a few minutes of your time? I'd like to know more."

Robert looked up from the card into the scrunched-up face before him.

"Was it possible?" he thought. "Could that story from two weeks ago have actually brought someone all the way from Palo Alto, California to Iowa to meet him? To see his machine?"

"Mama," he yelled over his shoulder toward the kitchen. "Better set another plate. We got a visitor."

Tommy felt the surprising grip of the old man begin to guide him off of the porch and into the rambler, where the smell of country-fried chicken wafted toward him.

"Maybe this trip wasn't a waste after all," he thought as he ambled toward the kitchen table.

= =

INDEX

27044178R00139

Made in the USA
Columbia, SC
25 September 2018